Realizing the Vision of Two-Way Immersion

Fostering Effective Programs and Classrooms

Printed in the United States of America
10 9 8 7 6 5 4 3 2 1

Professional Practice Series 5

Editorial/production supervision and substantive editing: Jeanne Rennie
Copyediting: EEI Communications, Inc.
Cover and interior design: EEI Communications, Inc., based on original designs by SAGARTdesign
Layout: EEI Communications, Inc.

ISBN 1-932748-61-X

The work reported in this book was supported in part by the following government agencies:

Office of Educational Research and Improvement, U.S. Department of Education
Educational Research and Development Centers Program
Cooperative Agreement Number R306A60001-96

National Institute for Child Health and Human Development
and
Institute of Education Sciences, U.S. Department of Education
Grant No. 5-P01-HD39530

The contents of this book do not necessarily represent the positions or policies of these agencies, and you should not assume endorsement by the federal government.

The research reported in this book was also made possible in part by a grant from the **Spencer Foundation.** The data presented, the statements made, and the views expressed are solely the responsibility of the authors.

Realizing the Vision of Two-Way Immersion

Fostering Effective Programs and Classrooms

Elizabeth R. Howard
Julie Sugarman

CENTER
FOR APPLIED
LINGUISTICS

DELTA SYSTEMS CO., INC.
Delta Publishing Company • Raven Tree Press

CAL CENTER
FOR APPLIED
LINGUISTICS

The Center for Applied Linguistics is a private nonprofit organization working to improve communication through better understanding of language and culture. Established in 1959, CAL has earned a national and international reputation for its contributions to the fields of bilingual education, English as a second language, foreign language education, dialect studies, literacy education, language policy, refugee orientation, and the education of linguistically and culturally diverse adults and children. CAL's staff of researchers and educators conduct research, design and develop instructional materials and language tests, provide technical assistance and professional development, conduct needs assessments and program evaluations, and disseminate information and resources related to language and culture. For more information about CAL, visit www.cal.org.

 **DELTA SYSTEMS CO., INC.**
Delta Publishing Company • Raven Tree Press

Delta Systems Co., Inc., is a publisher and distributor of English as a second language and foreign language materials. Since 1993, Delta has had a co-publishing agreement with the Center for Applied Linguistics. Joint CAL/Delta publications include the *Professional Practice Series,* additional professional reference books for language educators, and several sets of professional development materials for educators and paraprofessionals working with English language learners:

- *Enhancing English Language Learning in Elementary Classrooms*
- *Enriching Content Classes for Secondary ESOL Students*
- *What's Different About Teaching Reading to Students Learning English?*
- *Professional Development for Bilingual and ESL Paraprofessionals: The Aspire Curriculum Trainers Manual*

The Professional Practice Series

Teachers and administrators at all levels of education need ready access to clear and reliable information about effective educational practices. CAL's *Professional Practice Series* is designed to provide practitioners with current information on topics, trends, and techniques in language education. Each volume addresses a particular topic of interest to foreign language educators or to those who work with students learning English as a second language.

The initial chapters of each volume provide an overview of the topic, describing its scope and importance, summarizing what is known from research and practice, and identifying challenges and questions that remain to be addressed. The following chapters describe specific programs or instructional approaches that have been shown to be effective. The concluding chapters summarize key points in the book, provide recommendations for educators who wish to implement similar approaches, and offer suggestions for future discussion and research.

Through the *Professional Practice Series,* CAL strives to provide language educators with accessible and timely information, supported by theory and research, that will help them enhance and enrich their teaching and their programs.

Jeanne Rennie and Joy Kreeft Peyton, Series Editors
Center for Applied Linguistics
Washington, DC

Other Titles in the Professional Practice Series

Lessons Learned: Model Early Foreign Language Programs
English Language Learners with Special Education Needs:
    Identification, Assessment, and Instruction
Creating Access: Language and Academic Programs for Secondary
    School Newcomers
Language by Video: An Overview of Foreign Language Instructional
    Videos for Children

For more information about these titles and other publications from CAL, visit www.cal.org/resources/publications.html.

To my husband, Maurice, for your love, patience, encouragement, and support.

—Liz

To my parents, Robert and Joan, for instilling in me intellectualism, a passion for equity, and leadership.

—Julie

Table of Contents

Acknowledgments

This book incorporates findings from research projects that have taken place over the past 10 years. We have a long list of colleagues to whom we are profoundly grateful.

First, we would like to thank our CAL colleagues who have worked with us on these studies. Igone Arteagoitia and Cate Coburn have been tremendous assets to CAL's work in two-way immersion and the DeLSS study in particular. We are also grateful for the contributions of Christina Card, Lupe Hernandez-Silva, and Leo Vizcarra, as well as former colleagues Silvia Caglarcan, Martha Davis, Michael Loeb, Cathy McCargo, and Raquel Serrano.

We would also like to thank the research assistants who participated in the qualitative data collection at the programs profiled in this book: Louisa Aguirre-Baeza, John Evar Strid, and Ana Laura Treviño. Thanks also to Flo Decker, Kim Potowski, Patrick Proctor, and Libby Ware for their help in data collection for the CREDE study and to Jill Aller, Merton Bland, Justina Cooley, Kojo Johnson, Marialuz Castro Johnson, Cecilia Lewis, Erin McCabe, Solange Mecham, Alicia Sanderman, Stephanie Scott, Shelley Spaulding, Emma Trentman, Jennifer Tucker, Mercedes Valén, Marie-Colombe Wright, and Michelle Salazar for their work on the DeLSS study.

We are grateful for the ongoing mentoring we have received during our work on these studies, particularly from Diane August, Maggie Bruck, Grace Burkart, Donna Christian, Fred Genesee, Kris Gutiérrez, Kathryn Lindholm-Leary, Deborah Short, and Catherine Snow. For their help with statistical and methodological concerns, we would like to thank Gheorghe Doros, David Francis, Dorry Kenyon, Mohammed Louguit, Valerie Malabonga, Betsy McCoach, Judy Singer, and Herb Ware.

The quality of this book is much higher as a result of the careful editing of Jeannie Rennie, as well as feedback from Leslie Poyner and two anonymous external reviewers.

We are grateful to all of the past and present administrators and teachers in the schools and districts featured in this book:

- Carmen de la Cruz Scales, Evelyn Fernández, Ivonne Govea, Evelyn Manzano, Patricia Martinez, Ana Mosel, Marjorie Myers, Marleny Perdomo, Socorro Rojas, Miriam Stein, and Kathy Wills at Arlington Public Schools and Key Elementary School

- Maria Cabrera, Zoila García, Eva Helwing, Janet Nolan, Jill Sontag, Cheryl Urow, and Cindy Zucker at Chicago Public Schools and Inter-American Magnet School
- Peter Dittami, Ester de Jong, Minerva Gonzalez, Raquel Gordon, and Susan McGilvray-Rivet at Framingham Public Schools and Barbieri Elementary School
- Teresa Cortez, Anne Holder, Conchita Medina, Marina Miles, Nancy Ryan, Robert Schulte, and Micha Villarreal at Ysleta Independent School District and Alicia R. Chacón International School

Last, we are most indebted to the participating teachers and students, who very patiently tolerated all of our ongoing assessments and other interruptions over the multiple years of each study, and to the students' parents, who gave their consent and participated in data collection as well.

Chapter 1:
Setting the Context

Introduction

The development of bilingualism and biliteracy is one of the primary goals of two-way immersion (TWI) education, yet fostering their attainment can present a real challenge to teachers and administrators. External pressures, such as the greater use and status of English in the wider society and the current high-stakes atmosphere of standardized achievement testing in English, can work against the development of proficiency in another language. Internal challenges include identifying effective and appropriate strategies, materials, and assessments in both languages to use with integrated groups of students, who frequently have widely varying and sometimes competing educational needs. Additionally, the lack of district, state, or national standards for language and literacy attainment in the partner language (i.e., the non-English language) makes it difficult to fully assess the extent to which programs are attaining their goals of bilingualism and biliteracy development for all students.

However, the tremendous increase in the number of TWI programs since the late 1990s (Center for Applied Linguistics, 2006) has brought with it the emergence of a body of research addressing the success of the TWI model in meeting the academic needs of language majority and language minority children and providing evidence that students are achieving the goals of TWI. In a recent literature review, Howard, Sugarman, and Christian (2003) examined several large-scale longitudinal studies (Howard, 2003; Howard, Christian, & Genesee, 2003; Lindholm-Leary, 2001; Thomas & Collier, 1997, 2002) and dozens of small-scale studies that provide ample evidence of success of the TWI model while also pointing to some areas that deserve additional consideration as the model continues to be used and adapted.

This volume examines the development of bilingualism and biliteracy in elementary school students as informed by the emerging research base, identifying specific elements of school culture and instruction that can promote the achievement of bilingualism and biliteracy in TWI programs.

The Two-Way Immersion Model

TWI programs are a distinctive form of dual language education, with the following defining characteristics:

- They promote additive bilingualism by providing content and literacy instruction in English and the partner language (usually Spanish) for an extended period of time: minimally K–5, optimally K–12.
- Throughout the program, a minimum of 50% of instructional time is in the partner language.
- The program enrolls a balance of students who are native speakers of each (or both) of the two languages, preferably in a 50:50 ratio, but no more than two thirds of the students are native speakers of either language.
- The two groups of students are integrated for at least 50% of the instructional day.

Like all forms of dual language education (including developmental bilingual, heritage language, and foreign language immersion programs), which strive for high levels of bilingualism, biliteracy, and academic achievement for all students, TWI programs have four specific goals:

- Students will develop high levels of oral and written proficiency in their native language.
- Students will develop high levels of oral and written proficiency in their second language.
- Academic performance will be at or above grade level, regardless of the language of instruction.
- Students will demonstrate positive cross-cultural attitudes and behaviors.

Key findings from *Trends in Two-Way Immersion Education: A Review of the Research* (Howard, Sugarman, et al., 2003)

Academic Achievement

- Both native Spanish speakers and native English speakers in TWI programs perform as well as or better than their peers in other types of programs on both English and Spanish standardized achievement tests.
- Within TWI programs, native speakers tend to outperform second language learners; that is, native English speakers tend to score higher on English achievement tests, and native Spanish speakers tend to score higher on Spanish achievement tests.
- There is some indication of transfer of content knowledge from one language to the other, as students were sometimes instructed in one language and assessed in the other and still demonstrated grade-appropriate mastery of the content.

Language and Literacy Development

- Native Spanish speakers tend to be more balanced bilinguals than native English speakers.
- Students rated as balanced bilinguals with high levels of proficiency in both languages tend to outperform other students.
- There is some indication of transfer of literacy skills across languages when orthographies are similar.

Integration of Language Minority and Language Majority Students

- Merely grouping students together does not promote collaboration in and of itself.
- Students are helped by working together in integrated settings. Second language learners acquire vocabulary and syntax, while native speakers gain greater metalinguistic awareness through their language-brokering activities.
- There seem to be differences in peer interaction during Spanish instructional time and English instructional time, both in terms of focus and language use.
- Students have positive feelings toward themselves and others and have generally positive attitudes toward bilingualism and toward school.

The number of schools offering TWI programs has grown from 30 schools in the late 1980s (Lindholm, 1987) to 330 schools in 2006 (Center for Applied Linguistics, 2006). This growth has likely been motivated by the documented success of the program model, increased attention to the low academic performance and high dropout rate of Hispanic students in the United States (National Center for Education Statistics, 2002), and increasing interest in developing multilingualism in American students to help them succeed in the global economy.

With this growth has come a burgeoning of different approaches to implementing the model in accordance with local needs and resources. Programs differ, for example, in the percentage of time students are instructed in the partner language, in the language used for initial literacy instruction (i.e., the partner language, the native language, or both languages simultaneously), and in the extent to which students are separated (if ever) into homogeneous native language groups for targeted instruction. The two basic program types are called "90/10" and "50/50," referring to the ratio of Spanish to English instruction in the primary grades, although the precise ratio varies from school to school (Howard & Christian, 2002).

The criteria for successful TWI programs have been well established in the literature (Calderón & Minaya-Rowe, 2003; Cloud, Genesee, & Hamayan, 2000; Freeman, Freeman, & Mercuri, 2005; Howard & Christian, 2002; Howard, Lindholm-Leary, Sugarman, Christian, & Rogers, 2005; Lindholm, 1990; Soltero, 2004). In addition to the program-level features mentioned above, the literature supports an approach to literacy instruction that

- Balances teaching explicit phonemic and grammatical skills with opportunities for language development through reading and writing for meaningful purposes (Pressley, 2002)
- Uses sheltered instruction strategies (Echevarria, Vogt, & Short, 2004)
- Provides flexible grouping and differentiated instruction
- Offers active and cooperative learning practices (Cohen & Lotan, 1995; Slavin, 1995)
- Has a well-planned curriculum that provides explicit language arts instruction in both languages by the upper elementary grades
- Provides opportunities for the integration of language and academic content (Echevarria et al., 2004; Genesee, 1994; Swain, 1996)

CAL Studies of Two-Way Immersion Education

The Center for Applied Linguistics (CAL) conducted a 7-year study of TWI education funded by the U.S. Department of Education through the Center for Research on Education, Diversity & Excellence (CREDE). Two of the research goals of this study were to examine the effectiveness of TWI in promoting bilingualism, biliteracy, and academic achievement; and to document the characteristics of effective TWI learning environments. As part of this study, CAL researchers conducted a quantitative longitudinal study of the writing, reading, and oral language development of students in 11 TWI programs throughout the country and collected qualitative data on effective instructional practices from 4 exemplary programs.

Other CAL studies on TWI include a 5-year longitudinal study funded by the National Institute for Child Health and Human Development and the U.S. Department of Education through the Development of Literacy in Spanish Speakers (DeLSS) initiative. This study, Spelling as an Indicator of English Literacy Development, was a subproject of the DeLSS Acquiring Literacy in English research program. CAL also conducted a 2-year project, the Two-Way Immersion Teacher Research Collaborative, with funding from the Spencer Foundation.

The majority of the data in this book are from the four exemplary TWI programs identified in the 7-year CREDE study. Some of the data on the TWI program at Key Elementary School are from the two other CAL studies mentioned above. The qualitative data in chapters 4–6 are drawn primarily from focus groups, interviews with veteran teachers, interviews with school and district administrators, and observations of classrooms in the four schools, all conducted between spring 2000 and spring 2002 as part of the CREDE study. Each focus group of four to six teachers met twice with a trained research assistant who used a CAL-developed questionnaire to guide the discussion. The questions probed for information about successful instructional strategies in TWI classrooms, with special attention to language and literacy instruction provided through language arts and content lessons. Classroom observations were conducted with a focus on many of the same issues, as well as to look for evidence of the practices that were discussed in the focus groups. Using the constant comparison method (Glaser & Strauss, 1967), we reviewed our notes and transcripts multiple times, categorizing and coding data by reflecting on a combination of the words and actions of study participants as reflected in the transcripts, the themes that have been shown to be important in previous research on TWI and/or effective schools in general, and our own experiences in visiting these and other schools and collecting data for a number of studies on bilingualism and biliteracy development in TWI programs. This coding process led to the development of the key ideas that we put forth in this book about effective contexts for promoting bilingualism and biliteracy. The vignettes and quotes included in the book are drawn from the transcripts of the focus groups and the notes made by the observers.

The Four Focal Schools

As mentioned above, four schools were chosen for in-depth qualitative investigation:

- Alicia Chacón International School in El Paso, Texas
- Barbieri Elementary in Framingham, Massachusetts
- Inter-American Magnet School in Chicago, Illinois
- Francis Scott Key Elementary School in Arlington, Virginia

All four schools showed successful student language and literacy outcomes in the CAL studies mentioned above, as well as in previous CAL research (Christian, Montone, Lindholm, & Carranza, 1997; Howard & Christian, 1997) and in studies by other investigators (see page 11 for references). They have also demonstrated strong model fidelity and high levels of staff commitment and reflectiveness, which make them ideal candidates for qualitative investigation. Finally, these schools were chosen because they vary on a number of key features of TWI programs—including program model, approach to initial literacy instruction, student population, and geographical location—thus reinforcing our belief that there is no one right way to implement TWI programs and that a variety of approaches can be successful. A brief description of each school as it operated at the time of data collection is provided in the paragraphs that follow. Updated information about changes in the four programs since the period of data collection can be found in chapter 8. For those who seek additional information, extensive profiles of the four programs can be found in the works cited at the end of this chapter.

Alicia Chacón International School

El Paso, Texas, is home to a large number of TWI programs, including that of the Alicia Chacón International School in the Ysleta School District. This whole-school, K–8 magnet program began in 1995 as the district's first TWI program and currently enrolls students, who are selected by lottery, from all over the district. Alicia Chacón's program model is unusual in that it includes a third language component—Mandarin Chinese, German, Japanese, or Russian—for 10% of the school day at all grade levels. Students in the early grades receive 80% of their instruction in Spanish and 10% in English. The ratio of English-to-Spanish instruction gradually increases until roughly equal proportions of instructional time are provided in each of the two languages

Table 1.1: Overview of the Four Schools

Name	Location	Grades	Setting	Population	Average Mobility*
Alicia Chacón International School	El Paso, TX	K–8	Whole school	Predominantly Latino	5.7%
Barbieri Elementary School	Framingham, MA	K–5	Strand within a school	White/Latino	—
Inter-American Magnet School (IAMS)	Chicago, IL	PreK–8	Whole school	Multiracial	6.9%
Key Elementary School	Arlington, VA	K–5	Whole school	White/Latino	6.6%

*Average mobility between 2000 and 2002. Alicia Chacón and IAMS mobility rate from state school report card. Key information based on enrollment rates on state school report card. Barbieri information unavailable.

by fifth grade. The majority of students are Latino and are eligible for free or reduced-price lunch, and the language dominance of entering students is balanced among native English speakers, native Spanish speakers, and native bilinguals.

Barbieri Elementary School

Framingham, Massachusetts, began a TWI program at Barbieri Elementary School in 1990 in response to increasing social segregation of the school's bilingual students and decreasing enrollment of middle-class White students. Two first-grade teachers, with the support of school and district administrators, led the effort to turn one of Barbieri's transitional bilingual education strands into a TWI program, with two classes per grade level. (The school's general education strand also has two classes per grade level.) The TWI program later expanded into an additional elementary school and into one middle school and one high school. The program's student population is composed of relatively equal numbers of native English speakers, most of whom are White and do not qualify for free or reduced-price lunch, and native Spanish speakers, most of whom are Latino and do qualify for free or reduced-price lunch. The program is not classified as either 90/10 or 50/50 because the students receive different amounts of Spanish instruction depending on their native language. This "differentiated" program model at Barbieri separates students by native language for some language arts and content instruction and will be discussed more fully below.

Inter-American Magnet School

Inter-American Magnet School (IAMS) in Chicago is a whole-school, preK–8 program. It is one of the oldest TWI programs in the country; it started in 1975 with a grassroots effort by two bilingual parents who wanted their children to be educated bilingually. It began as a 50/50 program but later changed to an 80/20 program in which students receive 80% of their instruction in Spanish in the early grades, with English instruction increasing each year until a 50/50 ratio is reached by sixth grade. Because of a desegregation court ruling, the program is mandated to conduct its enrollment lottery by race/ethnicity rather than by native language, so there tend to be more native English speakers than native Spanish speakers. About two thirds of the students are Latino. Most of the other students are White or African American, with a very small number of Asians and Native Americans rounding out the student population. About half the students are eligible for free or reduced-price lunch.

Francis Scott Key Elementary School

The TWI program at Key Elementary School in Arlington, Virginia, began in 1986 as a gifted and talented program, but it is now open to all students. The whole-school program enrolls about 570 students, slightly more of whom are native English speakers than native Spanish speakers. The district has a second whole-school TWI program at the elementary level and continuation programs at the secondary level through course offerings in one middle school and one high school. Key Elementary has historically had roughly equal percentages of native Spanish speakers and native English speakers, but a current demographic shift in the district is resulting in a greater percentage of native English speakers entering the program. Slightly less than half the students, mostly native Spanish speakers, are eligible for free or reduced-price lunch. The program follows the 50/50 model at all grade levels, with native Spanish and English speakers integrated nearly 100% of the time.

Shared Vision and Cultures

Although there are significant differences among these four schools, they have all been effective at leading their students to achieve the TWI goals of bilingualism and biliteracy. They also share the very real challenges facing all TWI programs, such as limited resources; restrictive education policies; changing political conditions at the local, state, and national levels; and tremendous variation in the educational backgrounds and home language and literacy practices of their students.

What these four schools have in abundance is a school-wide vision. The CAL study revealed their staffs to be reflective, process oriented, and systemic in their approach to program improvement and professional development. These qualities are cited by the *Guiding Principles for Dual Language Education* (Howard, Lindholm-Leary, et al., 2005) as required for demonstrating exemplary alignment to best practices for effective programs (see also Lindholm-Leary, 2005). Another shared quality of these programs is that they combine a top-down and grassroots framework for reflection, training, and change. Strong leadership from teachers and administrators is responsive to the concerns of individuals and groups of stakeholders. Programs use expertise provided by outside consultants and research, but also consider how that advice plays out in their particular context. There will always be disagreements and compromise on the subtleties of decision making, but the actions of the program staff are based on a strong, unified philosophical orientation that defines the culture inside the school as well as how the school defines itself to the outside world. Finally, these programs demonstrate strong model fidelity, with a clear, consistent, and defensible model that is supported and carried out in all classrooms, yet that still allows teachers flexibility and the opportunity to play to their individual strengths.

About This Book

In this book, we look at effective TWI education through three lenses: the culture of **intellectualism,** the culture of **equity,** and the culture of **leadership.** We provide evidence of how these cultures function as organizing principles for the choices made—at both the program and the classroom level—that promote bilingualism and biliteracy among TWI students. While we believe that these three cultures contribute to successful academic and cross-cultural outcomes as well, our studies have focused on bilingualism and biliteracy development in particular, and we are therefore best able to comment on these outcomes.

On their own, program models, curricula, and instructional strategies are necessary but insufficient means to achieve the goals of academic achievement, bilingualism and biliteracy, and cross-cultural competence in two-way immersion. Unless the program fosters empowerment and demonstrates respect for students, staff, and parents through cultures of intellectualism, equity, and leadership, good design alone will not lead to good outcomes for student achievement. In effective programs, the interaction patterns among adults, between adults and children, and among children are all based on respect; serve to reinforce the cultural norms of intellectualism, equity, and leadership; and in the end, lead to the empowerment of all individuals and of the program as a whole.

In the chapters that follow, we provide evidence of exemplary practices in four schools at a particular moment in their history. Chapter 2 provides an overview of the instructional practices in each program, which are based on research and best practices in TWI settings. Chapter 3 provides empirical support for the selection of these four schools as exemplary TWI programs by presenting student outcomes in the areas of oral language, reading, and writing, and placing them in the context of the larger body of research on language and literacy development in dual language programs. Chapters 4, 5, and 6 provide examples of how the instructional strategies described in chapter 2 are used in effective programs to promote bilingualism and biliteracy through the cultures of intellectualism, equity, and leadership at both the program and classroom levels. Chapter 7 brings the ideas of intellectualism, equity, and leadership to life through the description of two instructional approaches developed by teachers in two of the programs profiled here, each of which exemplifies a number of the themes and strategies discussed in this book. The central ideas of the book are summarized

For more information about the four profiled schools:

Alicia Chacón

Calderón, M. E., & Minaya-Rowe, L. (2003). *Designing and implementing two-way bilingual programs: A step-by-step guide for administrators, teachers, and parents.* Thousand Oaks, CA: Corwin Press.

Howard, E. R. (2002). The Alicia Chacón International School: Portrait of an exemplary two-way immersion program. *NABE News, 25*(6), 19–22, 42–43.

Barbieri

de Jong, E. J. (2002). Effective bilingual education: From theory to academic achievement in a two-way bilingual program. *Bilingual Research Journal, 26*(1).

IAMS

Christian, D., Montone, C., Lindholm, K., & Carranza, I. (1997). *Profiles in two-way immersion education.* Washington, DC, and McHenry, IL: Center for Applied Linguistics and Delta Systems.

Kirk Senesac, B. V. (2002). *Two-way bilingual immersion: A portrait of quality schooling.* Bilingual Research Journal, *26*(1).

Potowski, K. (2002). *Language use in a dual immersion classroom: A sociolinguistic perspective.* Unpublished doctoral dissertation, University of Illinois, Urbana-Champaign.

Urow, C., & Sontag, J. (2001). *Creating community—Un mundo entero: The Inter-American experience.* In D. Christian & F. Genesee (Eds.), Bilingual education (pp. 11–26). Alexandria, VA: Teachers of English to Speakers of Other Languages.

Zucker, C. (1995). The role of ESL in a dual language program. *The Bilingual Research Journal, 19*(3&4), 513–523.

Key

Christian, D., Montone, C., Lindholm, K., & Carranza, I. (1997). *Profiles in two-way immersion education.* Washington, DC, and McHenry, IL: Center for Applied Linguistics and Delta Systems.

Rhodes, N. C., Christian, D., & Barfield, S. (1997). *Innovations in immersion: The Key School two-way model.* In R. K. Johnson & M. Swain (Eds.), *Immersion education: International perspectives* (pp. 265–283). New York: Cambridge University Press.

See also individual school profiles in CAL's *Directory of Two-Way Bilingual Immersion Programs* (www.cal.org/twi/directory).

in chapter 8, along with a postscript that provides updates on current happenings at each of the four programs. An appendix includes a study guide to facilitate the use of the book by groups of teachers for professional development purposes; to compare their approaches, strategies, and outcomes to those used in the four programs profiled here; and to discuss ways to strengthen and improve the development of bilingualism and biliteracy among students in their program.

Chapter 2:
Approaches to Instruction for Bilingualism and Biliteracy

Variety in Program Models

There are a number of model variations in TWI programs, including the ratio of Spanish instruction to English instruction in the primary grades, the content areas taught in each language, and the separation (or not) of students into groups by ability and/or native language for targeted instruction. These variations are generally based on logistical, pedagogical, or political concerns, and any number of variations can be successful in a given context (Howard & Christian, 2002; Howard, Sugarman, et al., 2003). The four programs featured in this book use a variety of basic models (two use a modified 90/10, one is 50/50, and one differentiated). Additionally, the programs use three different approaches to initial literacy instruction in the first 2 or 3 years of school: One program provides initial literacy instruction in Spanish for all students, two programs have each group of students begin literacy instruction in their native language, and one program begins literacy instruction in both languages for all students.

The programs also differ in whether students are ever grouped by native language and in their use of English as a second language (ESL) and Spanish as a second language (SSL) instruction. In TWI programs that have designated ESL and/or SSL support, this type of instruction is offered primarily in the early grades and consists of targeted second language instruction with groups of students who are separated by native language. Some TWI schools continue to use targeted pullout ESL and SSL for small groups of students (both newcomers and those who continue to struggle with their second language) in the upper elementary grades. Table 2.1 summarizes the program models used in each school, and details about these approaches are provided below.

Table 2.1: Summary of Program Models

School	Model	Language of Initial Literacy	Language of Content Areas	ESL/SSL Instruction by a Specialist
Alicia Chacón International School	Spanish dominant (80/10/10 – modified 90/10)	Spanish	Math/science in Spanish, social studies in English	None
Barbieri Elementary School	Differentiated; amount of Spanish instruction varies by native language	Native language	Math in English, science and social studies alternate languages by unit	All students receive K–3, targeted thereafter
Inter-American Magnet School (IAMS)	Spanish dominant (80/20 – modified 90/10)	Native language	All content in Spanish K–4, science in English 5–8	All students receive K–1, targeted thereafter
Key Elementary School	Balanced (50/50)	Both	Math/science in Spanish, social studies in English	ESL K–5 for students who qualify for services

Program Model and Language of Initial Literacy Instruction

Among our four focal schools, Alicia Chacón is the closest to a classic 90/10 model, as it provides the most consistent use of Spanish in the primary grades, as well as the greatest amount of student integration. Initial literacy instruction is provided in Spanish to all students, with formal English literacy introduced to all students in the third grade. Oral language and literacy development in a third language also take place within the 10% of the day spent in one of four languages (Mandarin Chinese, German, Japanese, or

Russian). Science and math are taught in Spanish at all grade levels (K–8). Language arts lessons are thematically linked across and integrated into subject areas. Students are never separated into homogeneous native language groups for literacy or content instruction, nor are they provided with targeted ESL/SSL pullout instruction.

IAMS separates students in the primary grades by native language for initial literacy instruction and for targeted instruction in their second language. Formal second language literacy is introduced after first language literacy development is well under way, with the decision made on a student-by-student basis, but by second grade at the latest. IAMS is similar to Alicia Chacón in that the majority of instructional time for all students is provided in Spanish in the primary grades. The only instruction provided in English in Grades K–4 is language arts for native English speakers and ESL for native Spanish speakers. All other subjects are taught in Spanish to heterogeneous groups. Despite their lack of formal literacy instruction in Spanish in the primary grades, native English speakers are able to keep pace with content lessons through the supports they receive during targeted SSL instruction, as well as through the use of hands-on activities, thematic instruction, and language/content integration that initiates second language literacy in an informal, highly contextualized way. Starting in second grade, students also remain in heterogeneous groups for all literacy instruction. In fifth grade, as the program moves toward a 50/50 instructional ratio of Spanish to English, science instruction is switched to English.

The program model at Barbieri is likewise based on developing initial literacy in the students' native language. Students are separated by native language for the entire morning component, receiving language arts and math instruction through their native language, as well as targeted second language instruction. Native English and native Spanish speakers are integrated in the afternoon for science and social studies, which are taught in both languages on an alternating-unit basis (e.g., in science, a unit on the solar system in Spanish might be followed by a unit on plants in English). In the homogenous language arts classes, the time devoted to native language literacy versus development of oral second language skills is flexible, varying according to the needs of each cohort. In Grades K–2, students receive 70% of instruction in their native language; by third grade, they are increasingly integrated and the English/Spanish instructional ratio for all students is closer to 50/50.

Because it is unusual, an additional comment about Barbieri's model is warranted. The leaders involved in planning Barbieri's program chose this model because of a belief that native English speakers coming to Barbieri with limited preliteracy skills might benefit more by having initial literacy and math instruction in their native language. Teachers were also concerned that integrated Spanish language arts in the early grades would be watered down for the benefit of the native English speakers, which would be detrimental to the native Spanish speakers. (For additional details on the model and the rationale, see de Jong, 2002, and chapter 5 of this volume.) The model is currently undergoing further review based on student outcomes and feedback from teachers and parents, and it is going to change to an 80/20 model in fall 2007 (see chapter 8). This type of data-driven change reinforces the importance of ongoing reflection on all key instructional issues.

At Key, all students develop literacy skills in both languages simultaneously, and instructional time is divided equally between the two languages at all grade levels. One hour of English language arts instruction takes place in small groups divided by ability levels, allowing students to work with either their classroom teacher or a resource teacher according to their needs. Spanish language arts and all content instruction are delivered in heterogeneous classes. Social studies and language arts are taught in English; science, math, and a smaller language arts component are taught in Spanish at all grade levels (K–5). Increasing the amount of time and resources spent on language arts in Spanish has been a priority for the school. Whereas students in English language arts classes are grouped by ability, Spanish language arts is taught to the entire, heterogeneous class. All students work on similar skills, but individual assignments are tailored to the student's level in Spanish. This requires greater attention to differentiation on the part of the teacher than is the case in English, which is particularly challenging given time constraints of a 50/50 program. At this time, there are not enough additional resource teachers to allow for teacher-facilitated small group instruction in Spanish.

ESL/SSL Instruction in Homogenous Native-Language Groups

Differentiated instruction—instruction that is tailored to the levels and needs of individual learners—is an important concept in TWI education. Increasingly, more TWI programs are making program model choices that separate students by language or ability, as discussed above. At three of the four profiled schools (Alicia Chacón does not separate students by language or offer

ESL/SSL pullout services), both classroom teachers and resource teachers play an important role in providing this targeted instruction.

During one hour of their English language arts block, students at Key are grouped by ability (as determined by test scores and teacher observation) and may work in a group with their classroom teacher, a reading teacher, a special education teacher, or an ESL teacher. (This pullout support is available at whatever grade a student qualifies for services.) One of the ESL teachers stated in a focus group that she tries to pick reading material for her students that reflects what they are learning in the content areas, particularly in social studies, which is taught in English. She communicates regularly with the classroom teachers to support their instruction and to inform her own instruction. She wants her students to see a clear connection to their other language arts work and their work in the content areas. Spanish language arts is taught by the classroom teacher in the whole-class setting. Although the school does occasionally have access to additional specialists in Spanish to work with small groups of students, there is generally no pullout SSL support for native English speakers.

As mentioned earlier, students at IAMS receive some language arts instruction in homogenous native language groups. In kindergarten and Grade 1, all students receive targeted ESL or SSL instruction in small groups during their language arts time with their classroom teacher. Beginning in Grade 2, a second language support pullout program is provided for new arrivals to the program and for students who are having problems acquiring English or Spanish as a second language. The ESL and SSL pullout teachers work with small groups of 4 to 10 students on a flexible schedule using a literature-based approach to teach vocabulary and language structures. An early intervention reading teacher also works with small groups of struggling students in first through third grades in addition to their regular language arts time.

At Barbieri, in addition to ESL and SSL components of the regular language arts block in the primary grades (during the time that students are separated by native language), the school has both ESL and SSL teachers who work with groups of students needing extra help in their second language. The ESL teacher sees students from Grades 1–5 in small groups, focusing on oral language development in Grade 1 and on reading and writing starting in Grade 2. The SSL teacher focuses on Grades K–3, reinforcing content concepts in Grades K–1 and beginning reading and grammar instruction in Grade 2. Both coordinate their lessons with the classroom teachers' language arts and content lessons.

As a Spanish-dominant or modified 90/10 school, Alicia Chacón does not separate students into homogeneous native language groups or incorporate targeted ESL or SSL into its model. All students are taught to read initially in Spanish, so that the native Spanish speakers can model and provide support for the native English speakers, for whom the "full immersion" model allows ample time for second language development. Both groups then move together into formal English language arts in third grade, as they continue to receive Spanish literacy instruction. One of the advantages of the 90/10 model is that Spanish is the first language of literacy development for all students, and English is the second. This model offers fewer logistical challenges than the model in which initial literacy instruction must be coordinated across two languages and for both native speakers and second language learners.

Important Considerations for Model Choices

The wide diversity in program models and approaches to language distribution and initial literacy development described here, as well as the diversity in models we have seen in other programs, brings up several important points for teachers and administrators to consider as they design and reflect on their own programs. First, whatever program model and approach to initial literacy are selected, the choices must produce a coherent whole that makes sense internally and matches the program's vision and goals. There is very little guidance from research on which combination of approaches is best (Lindholm-Leary, 2005). However, some studies indicate that for both native English speakers and native Spanish speakers, providing the majority of primary grade instruction in Spanish improves Spanish language and literacy outcomes without compromising ultimate attainment in English language or literacy ability (Lindholm-Leary & Howard, in press). The choice of program model and approach to initial literacy also depends on factors such as the availability of bilingual staff, the constraints of mandated curricula, and judgments about whether the needs of native English speakers and native Spanish speakers will be met. Tools like the *Dual Language Program Planner* (Howard, Olague, & Rogers, 2003) and the *Guiding Principles for Dual Language Education* (Howard, Lindholm-Leary, et al., 2005) can help guide decisions that lead to coherent programs.

Second, an important—and sometimes overlooked—component of a model that separates students by native language for initial literacy but provides content instruction to all students in both languages is the inclusion of language arts instruction for each group of students in their second language as well (as both Barbieri and IAMS do). If a program is committed to developing formal literacy in students' native language before introducing formal literacy instruction in the second language, but students are expected to use literacy skills in the subject areas taught in their second language, they need targeted vocabulary, oral language, and literacy development in their second language along with sheltered instruction and integrated language objectives within content lessons. Another caution is that if students are taught for a significant portion of the day in their first language only, it is unlikely that native English speakers will have at least 50% of their instruction in Spanish, which is cited in the literature as a necessary feature of two-way immersion (Cloud et al., 2000; Howard & Christian, 2002; Lindholm-Leary, 2001). For example, if 30% of instruction is provided in the students' native language and all other time is divided equally between the two native languages, native English speakers will receive only 35% of their overall instruction in Spanish. This is likely to seriously compromise their ability to participate in academic activities in Spanish in the upper elementary grades, when the cognitive and linguistic demands become greater.

Finally, the approach needs to be consistent within and across grades, as attention to model fidelity is an important component of achieving the goals of bilingualism and biliteracy (Howard, Lindholm-Leary, et al., 2005; Lindholm-Leary, 2001, 2005). Consistency does not necessarily mean doing exactly the same thing at every grade level, but it does mean following through on key principles of the chosen program model in a logical and thoughtful way at each grade level. As we will demonstrate throughout this book, having a clearly defined model that all teachers understand, support, and implement is as important to the continued success of the program as the initial decisions about the program design.

Instruction for Bilingualism and Biliteracy

Several recent books describe effective ways to organize and deliver instruction for students in dual language programs (Calderón & Minaya-Rowe, 2003; Cloud et al., 2000; Freeman et al., 2005; Soltero, 2004). They draw on an extensive literature on instruction for second language learners (e.g., Echevarria et al., 2004; Genesee, Lindholm-Leary, Saunders, & Christian, 2006) and foreign language learners (e.g., Curtain & Dahlberg, 2003). When teachers in the CAL focus groups were asked about the strategies they use for teaching language and literacy skills, the themes that emerged were very similar to what is discussed in that literature: balanced literacy (using both skills-based and whole-language approaches), cooperative instruction, student-centered learning, a focus on strategies that can be used across the content areas and across languages, thematic units, and the integration of language and content instruction. Because these concepts are so widely discussed, we will not attempt to provide exhaustive insight into the particularities of the instructional strategies used by the many classroom teachers involved in our studies. Instead, the findings presented in this section serve three purposes:

- To provide empirical support for the position that effective programs have teachers that use these strategies
- To illuminate teachers' perceptions of how and why they use these strategies
- To provide a background for what instruction looks like in TWI classrooms, setting the stage for the vignettes in the rest of the book

Activities and Techniques for Developing Literacy Skills

TWI programs have historically favored whole-language approaches to literacy instruction for two reasons. First, TWI education gained strength in the late 1980s and early 1990s, when the whole-language movement was also increasing in popularity (Lindholm-Leary, 2001). Second, the teaching of language through academic content rather than in isolation as a discrete skill was a foundational principle of Canadian foreign language immersion, on which TWI was partially based (Genesee, 1987). Literacy instruction in both English and Spanish in the early two-way programs was often skewed more to literature-based, content-integrated approaches that avoided the explicit teaching of skills like phonics and spelling (Lindholm-Leary, 2001). In recent years, TWI programs have shifted, along with mainstream educational programs, to a more balanced approach, including the teaching of phonics and explicit language arts, while still incorporating whole-language principles such as thematic language and content units, using authentic literature, and focusing on comprehension skills (Lindholm-Leary, 2005; Pérez, 2004).

Several of the teachers in the focus groups expressed an emphasis on balance within their literacy approach. One Key teacher noted that "you have to use your whole bag of tricks [with regard to literacy development] because kids learn in different ways. And you don't want a child who can decode but not comprehend." A primary-grades IAMS teacher echoed this sentiment, saying that "students react better to a variety of approaches. Some understand with phonics, while others need [different strategies]. Different learning styles demand different approaches."

Overall, language arts instruction in the primary grades combines a skills approach, where specific phonemic or grammatical rules are explicitly taught, with a chance to engage in creative reading and writing activities that are engaging and connected to meaningful texts. Both Key and Barbieri emphasize the use of centers during language arts time, where students engage in both independent and cooperative literacy activities, as well as readers and writers workshops that have a thematic tie-in to their content lessons. IAMS and Alicia Chacón teachers in the focus groups particularly noted their use of trade books/authentic literature and thematic instruction, incorporating a variety of reading activities and mini-lessons around a single topic. For example, at Alicia Chacón, the primary teachers use literature that has a thematic tie-in to their other units of study as well as to the letter they're teaching. Kindergarten students might learn a for araña [spider], then read a book about spiders.

The following vignette, which occurred in a Spanish reading group in a second-grade classroom at IAMS, provides an example of this type of balanced literacy instruction in the primary grades.

The students who were going to read with the teacher gathered at a round table. The name of the book was Una sorpresa para Zorro [A Surprise for Zorro]. The teacher introduced the book by having the students look at the front of the book and the title. She asked them to predict what the book would be about. The students thought from the picture on the cover that the book was going to be about a dog named Zorro. She then asked them to open the book and look at the pictures and guess again. After the students had looked at all the pictures, she asked if they still thought the dog was Zorro. The students had changed their minds.

The teacher then had the students start to read the story, while she observed them and helped them as necessary. When she saw that they were reading without understanding, she stopped them and said, "Vamos a leer algunas palabras juntos [We're going to read some words together]." She had the students divide the word pulgoso [full of fleas] into syllables and talked about the meaning. She had them start reading again, instructing them to put their fingers under the words and to read aloud. When the students read, "***Encontró*** *perro pulgoso fue a su casa* [**(He/She/You) found** flea-ridden dog went home]" instead of "***Entonces*** *perro pulgoso fue a casa* [**Then** the flea-ridden dog went home]," she asked them, "*¿Tiene sentido eso?* [Does that make sense?] *Tiene que leer lo que está en la página* [You have to read what's on the page]." She helped the students divide *entonces* [then] into syllables and to then read the entire sentence correctly.

A little further on, the students confused capital *I* for small *l*. She explained to them that the capital *I* sometimes looks just like the small *l* and that they had to figure out which was the right one according to what made sense. *"Si no se entiende lo que está leyendo, no vale la pena leerlo* [If you don't understand what you're reading, it's not worth the trouble to read it]." She asked them some comprehension questions about the story, "*¿Qué metió en la caja amarilla?* [What did they put in the yellow box?]" *and* "*¿Adónde va?* [Where is he going?]."

Later the students read, "*Cada uno de los animales luego con una mascota* [Each one of the animals later with a pet]" substituting *luego* [later] for *llegó* [arrived]. The teacher said, "*¿Suena bien eso?* [Does that sound right?]." She pointed out that the first letter is the double *ll* and helped them figure out the word. The students went on reading. She helped a student use his finger to follow along while he was reading, since he was not doing it on his own. She used the white board to help the students divide the word *sabrosa* [tasty]. She asked the students to make a prediction about what would happen next in the story by asking, "*¿Quiere que su mascota le pica a Zorro?* [Does he want his pet to bite Zorro?]." She saw that they were running out of time and said they would finish reading the story the next time they had reading.

As students move into the upper grades, language arts instruction at all four schools focuses on comprehension strategies, such as making inferences and using cognates, and higher level skills, such as understanding how authors develop characters and mood in their writing. Teachers continue to engage the students in reading and writing activities connected to their thematic units, such as journaling, surveying, and creating character maps. Students in the upper grades often engage in extended cooperative activities, such as writers workshops and peer editing.

Developing vocabulary is an important component of language development at all grade levels. The upper elementary teachers at IAMS described their approach to vocabulary development as drawing on content areas and using techniques like prediction to engage students' higher order thinking skills. Vocabulary-building activities that follow from this approach include constructing meanings of new words by asking students to determine the likely part of speech and meaning of a word based on its context and then looking up the word in the dictionary to confirm or correct their predictions, or giving students a list of 10 words from which they predict what a story using those words might be about. To capitalize on students' bilingual competencies, teachers encourage them to use cognates, drawing attention to the fact that if they know the word in one language, they may also know it in the other. Several studies have found this approach to be useful with native Spanish speakers in particular (Carlo et al., 2004; Hancin-Bhatt & Nagy, 1994; Jiménez, García, & Pearson, 1996; Nagy, García, Durgunoglu, & Hancin-Bhatt, 1993).

Finally, error correction is a common concern of immersion teachers, and this is an area where a balanced approach that employs both indirect (through modeling) and direct (through explicit instruction) approaches is most effective. When students are working in their second language, there is frequently a tension between correcting them in order to prevent the fossilization of errors and letting errors go so as not to impede communication or tax or embarrass the student. At Alicia Chacón, the primary grade teachers spoke about the need to encourage students when they are working in their second language and to acknowledge their successes while constantly modeling the language for them. Their feeling, common to many primary immersion teachers, is that in the early grades, it is most important to promote an open and flexible environment where students feel comfortable using their second language. In this regard, providing indirect correction through modeling is the preferred approach. This feeling was echoed by primary teachers at Key. They added, however, that they provided explicit correction of errors when there were class-wide problems. This approach was shared by teachers at other schools. When an error was noticeable among a majority of students, it became the focus of a mini-lesson, and from that point forward, students were held accountable for its correct use. Similarly, Alicia Chacón teachers at the middle school level discussed the need to provide more explicit error correction to students and also to help them understand language variation and different registers, so they could determine the difference between social and academic language and when it is appropriate to use each.

Integrative Approaches to Instruction

TWI teachers need to be very efficient in coordinating and scaffolding instruction across the two program languages, while still being sure that students have sufficient opportunities to engage new content in multiple ways. Integrating language and content and giving students multiple opportunities to hear, speak, read, and write about new content across the curriculum takes a great deal of planning and coordination, but was cited by the teachers in our focus groups as a fundamental principle of their instruction.

Teaching Through Multiple Modalities and Thematic Units

One of the recurring themes in the focus group discussions about instructional strategies was teaching through multiple modalities and multiple contexts. As one teacher pointed out, different students have different learning needs, even beyond differences in language proficiency, and will "react better to a variety of approaches." For language learners, the use of multiple modalities (e.g., listening, singing, drawing, writing) is a key sheltered instructional strategy (see Echevarria et al., 2004) because it offers students multiple opportunities to understand the meaning of new material. One second-grade Spanish teacher offered this illustration of these strategies:

> I begin by giving them an overview of what they're going to learn so they know where they're going to go. I will typically kick it off with a song, a poem, or a chant that I created that contains words and grammar forms that are going to be cornerstones for concept development later on. So they might know two words of a sentence that I'm saying, but because I'm gesturing, showing meaning, and embedding what I'm saying in the environment with the meaning around me, they begin to understand. I don't translate anything; I shelter the environment [and] make references [using] voice intonation, gestures, props, all those things to help them understand.

A number of classes we observed utilized these multiple modalities within a single lesson. For example, in one first-grade Key classroom, a read-aloud was followed by an activity that incorporated speaking, drawing pictures, and writing in order to retell part of the story. In this way, teachers can differentiate instruction so that students who are struggling will have enough repetition and exposure through multiple activities to understand the new content in the lesson, while the more advanced students can do additional or more difficult activities related to the topic to enhance their skills.

The principle of using multiple modalities within a single lesson is related to the use of thematic and cross-disciplinary units, which gives students maximum exposure to the academic vocabulary and concepts that they need to learn. Through thematic units, teachers can also scaffold language and content concepts across the two program languages, which is especially important for programs like Key that separate languages by curricular area (e.g., math and science in Spanish, and social studies in English). Lessons are not repeated in both program languages, but the same language and literacy skills can be reinforced through various activities done in the different content areas. For example, a Spanish language arts unit on figurative language taught through proverbs could be extended and reinforced during social studies instruction in English that includes the reading of *Aesop's Fables* during a study of ancient Greece. (See the *Two-Way Immersion Toolkit* at www.cal.org/twi/toolkit for the lesson plan and video segments related to the co-planning and delivery of the lesson described here, as well as a number of other model lessons that use the various strategies discussed in this chapter.)

Integrating Language and Content

Planning for language development within content lessons is a crucial and challenging aspect of lesson planning for TWI classrooms, especially when students' language abilities do not match the materials available in a particular content area. One primary teacher stated that "it's a lot easier to integrate the science and social studies themes in second grade than it is in first grade, because you really struggle to get the students to start reading in first grade and you can't find resources that are at their level. In second grade, where the students are already better readers, it's a lot easier to integrate." Second language learners need support with new vocabulary and language structures in those materials, which can be provided through previews, mini-lessons, visuals, and adapted texts (Echevarria et al., 2004).

The upper-grades teachers at IAMS stated that the integration of language and content through thematic teaching is an important part of their instruction. In fourth grade, the curriculum is arranged according to thematic units, and language arts are taught almost entirely through the content areas. The teacher gives mini-lessons on language arts, focusing on specific skills that will be incorporated into the thematic unit. For example, in one fourth-grade class, the teacher chose to teach the Spanish conditional during a unit on the rain forest, integrating the grammar lesson of the subjunctive tense into the thematic unit: *"Si yo fuera un jaguar...."* ["If I were a jaguar ... (this is what I would do)"]. She found that because the students really enjoyed learning about the rain forest, they were motivated to use and improve their skills in the language used for instruction. The literature that was chosen also had clear thematic ties to the unit. An extended example of this integration is presented in Jill Sontag and Cheryl Urow's example of Fascinating Facts and Remarkable Reports in chapter 7 of this book.

Differentiating Instruction and Grouping in Integrated Classrooms

As is the case in other types of educational settings, TWI students' language and literacy development is tested regularly using standardized measures for purposes of accountability and promotion. Teachers also track their students' development through formative assessment, for example, by having students read individually and recording their observations of the students' performance. (For examples, see the oral language and writing rubrics designed by TWI teachers in Arlington, Virginia, at www.cal.org/twi/rubrics, as well as the model lessons in the *Two-Way Immersion Toolkit* at www.cal.org/twi/toolkit.) This enables teachers to see what cues each student is using and build on those, while drawing their attention to issues they need to teach more extensively or explicitly.

Unlike teachers in other settings, however, immersion teachers must either evaluate students' progress in two languages (at separate times, during the designated instructional time in each language) or communicate closely with the partner teacher who provides instruction through the other language. Key teachers noted specifically that their success in meeting individual students' needs was due to a lot of record keeping and communication among the various teachers and specialists, which enabled them to keep track of students' literacy and academic development. Administrators in the district where Key is located have noted that clarifying expectations for language proficiency in English and Spanish is one of their priorities for the two-way program in the district (Forbes-Ullrich & Perdomo, 2005).

Several teachers in the focus groups said that when working with their whole class, they tried to teach to the level of the highest achieving students while using sheltering strategies and peer assistance to support the struggling students and recent arrivals. When students are grouped heterogeneously by native language and ability level, instruction can be made flexible through self-paced activities, cooperative groupings, and instruction that is responsive to ongoing student assessment. Thematic units that incorporate language and content objectives and include a variety of activities around a central theme allow students to work at their highest level of ability, and allow teachers to regroup students based on their needs for any particular kind of task. According to a teacher at IAMS,

> Teachers have expectations for individual students within the thematic unit and expect them to live up to them. The activities are not focused on lectures, but allow students to learn at their own pace and do enough activities at their level to understand the material. There is a lot of individualized focus and mini-lessons that focus on the needs of specific students. We shoot higher than the kids' ability, and then we support the kids to reach that level.

Teachers at IAMS report that students have high listening and comprehension skills in both languages, but activities and expectations are differentiated at the level of "doing individual work and the amount and quality of the second language they are able to produce." Teachers in the focus groups also stated that their response to student errors depends on the stage of language development of the student; for example, they generally don't correct errors in oral language for second language speakers in the earlier stages of language acquisition.

With regard to different expectations for different students, a second-grade Spanish teacher at Barbieri said,

> My instruction varies by ability. I do cooperative groupings when I'm going to do any small-group instruction, and I use a lot of sheltered language and TPR [Total Physical Response]. ... Using those techniques and theories, I can really differentiate instruction through the questions that I use. I don't bring the standards down for students who need more help; I keep the standards high, and elicit from everyone what they can give me. I try to raise up the floor versus bringing down the ceiling, I guess is the way I could describe it. So if I'm reading a big book to the group and one child is still at the very early receptive stage—understands everything but can't really speak

spontaneously—maybe that child can come up and find a picture in the book and then repeat the word. And maybe the next child can respond orally, and the third child can make a prediction. So I'm keeping the content, but differentiating instruction that way. Then I put them in cooperative groups so that they can use one another as resources.

Alicia Chacón teachers reported that they, too, rely on the students supporting and learning from each other. Sometimes the teachers form groups that are heterogeneous by language dominance or whatever configuration is needed to accomplish the particular task. In fact, the teachers reported that "the bigger challenge is to teach to one homogenous group. With both language groups in one classroom, the students use each other for communication and clarification."

Modeling and Helping Students Become Independent Learners

Because the ability to work both cooperatively and independently is required of students in immersion programs, teachers need to model and instruct students in learning strategies that they can use on their own, as well as appropriate strategies for asking for and offering help. One IAMS teacher reflected,

One thing that I find just wonderful about the students here is that they want so much … and will use whatever means they have to help each other. And if that requires them to do it in English to do a good job, they'll do it. So we have to try to work harder on giving them more incentive to use Spanish in the process of helping each other.… I've been working a little more this year with strategies on how, without using English, they can help each other. But I have to model them for them. I've stopped many times and instead of getting someone to [explain to] somebody else in English, [I've used another strategy].…

One of the words this week was *rolling*, and [an English dominant] boy came up to me: "How do you say rolling?" Because he was writing a story about a monster whose eyeballs fell off.… So I made an effort to actually do the modeling of what I wanted them to do. I knew that there was a child here who could explain it in Spanish. So I thought of somebody and then I said, "Okay, how do you say it?" I pretended I didn't know how to say it, which was very effective, because some of the students said, "Teacher doesn't know how to say 'rolling'!" So I said, "Okay ... could you please tell [him]: How do you say it when a dog plays tricks on the floor and he's going like that. That action." And she couldn't get it. This is in Spanish. "How about if you're at the park and you're playing and you go like this." I was trying to avoid saying the word. I wanted to get her mind thinking in Spanish, because she has lived those things in Spanish. She has a dog. She's gone to the park. She knows all of those things. I just needed to get the context in her mind so she wouldn't think English. It's so easy to think English because of what they see on TV, how they play with each other. But if you can get those children to think of a child who has lived those experiences in Spanish, it's automatic for them. And it was automatic. She said, "I know." She had warmed up already. She just blurted it out, *"Rodando, ya sé, ya sé."*

Teachers also described how they model ways that students can avoid asking for a translation or using a bilingual dictionary. During read-aloud time, one teacher went from stopping and asking for a translation when she found a word she thought the students might not know to modeling ways of finding the meaning of the unknown word from the context, all in the target language. Additionally, teachers encourage the students to use cognates, noting that this type of instruction was one of the few situations in which they would code-switch between English and the partner language. Occasional, intentional use of both program languages is supported by researchers who find academic and social benefits (Cummins, 2006; Hadi-Tabassum, 2006).

At a broader level, reading is a skill that is transferable across different domains and even across languages. One IAMS teacher puts an emphasis on teaching multiple reading strategies, calling each one "the reading strategy of the week." Similarly, by explicitly teaching strategies, one Key teacher noted that "the kids learn strategies so that they can apply them on their own. They can self-monitor and they don't always need me right there.... Often it's just asking them, 'What do you need to do?' instead of saying, 'You need to reread' so they learn to internalize it." Finally, a Barbieri teacher stated, "They need to learn strategies, how to express themselves in writing. They are learning how to learn and self-perpetuating learning. Helping students to internalize [a strategy] after the teacher models it was a big shift, not just in this district but also around the country."

Conclusion

All of the above program design choices and instructional strategies constitute individual features of effective classrooms and schools (Lindholm-Leary, 2005). They demonstrate that the paths to bilingualism and biliteracy differ, both within schools (across the two groups of native language speakers) and across schools, although the desired ends are the same. For the most part, the instructional strategies used in the four focal schools are similar, but they may play out differently in each context, depending on program model, demographics, and state or local testing constraints, among other factors.

Despite some differences in approach among the four schools, the outcome data in the next chapter demonstrate that they are all effective in promoting bilingualism and biliteracy among their students. However, not all of the outcome data reflect the ideal ends. There frequently are achievement gaps between native English speakers and native Spanish speakers in both languages, as well as imbalance in first and second language proficiency for individual students, particularly native English speakers. These profiled schools are not perfect, but they do produce compelling language and literacy outcomes in spite of their struggles with the very real political, logistical, and social challenges that all TWI programs face.

Chapter 3:
Bilingualism and
Biliteracy Attainment
in Two-Way Immersion
Programs

Introduction

Attainment of high levels of bilingualism and biliteracy is one of the three primary goals of TWI education (Howard & Christian, 2002; Lindholm-Leary, 2001, 2005). As such, it has been the topic of a fair amount of TWI research, including several large-scale, longitudinal studies (Howard, Christian, et al., 2003; Lindholm-Leary, 2001; Thomas & Collier, 1997, 2002), as well as a number of smaller-scale studies that have generally focused on student outcomes for a single TWI program or district (e.g., Bae & Bachman, 1998; Cazabon, Lambert, & Hall, 1993; Gort, 2001; Ha, 2001; Pérez, 2004; Potowski, 2002. (See Howard, Sugarman, et al., 2003, for a review of this research.) The purpose of this chapter is to contribute to this research base by presenting student outcome data from the four focal programs.

In the sections that follow, we provide school-specific findings for native Spanish speakers and native English speakers in the domains of oral language, reading, and writing. We then discuss these findings in the broader context of relevant research to date. Native language designations are based on school records, which in turn were based on intake testing and home language surveys conducted at students' entry in their respective programs (by first grade, as a requirement of participation in both of our longitudinal studies). Our findings are based on both longitudinal data that demonstrate performance of TWI students over time in these domains, and cross-sectional comparison data that indicate the relative performance of TWI students compared to other students in the district and/or state. Data for Alicia Chacón, Barbieri, and IAMS come from the CREDE study, whereas data for Key come from the spelling study, both described in chapter 1. In both cases, measures of oral language, reading, and writing were administered at multiple time points over a period of 3 years (CREDE) or 4 years (spelling study).

The development of bilingualism and biliteracy was a key focus of the CREDE study. However, because of the lack of available measures to assess the first and second language or literacy ability of both native English speakers and native Spanish speakers, the CREDE study relied on project-developed measures that are not standardized. The oral language measure is an analytic rubric with a scale of 0 to 5 points. There are two components of the rubric, conversational fluency and grammar, each of which has four subcomponents. Each subcomponent is rated on a scale of 0 to 5, and a total score is computed by averaging all eight subcomponent scores. Oral language data were collected from a stratified random subsample of students at the end of third grade and the end of fifth grade, using a pair interview format based on the *Student Oral Proficiency Assessment (SOPA)* (Thompson, Boyson, & Rhodes, 2001).

The narrative writing measure is also an analytic rubric with a structure and content similar to those of the oral language rubric. The writing rubric has three components—composition, grammar, and mechanics—each of which has four subcomponents. As with the oral language rubric, each subcomponent is rated on a scale of 0 to 5, and a total score is computed by averaging all 12 subcomponent scores. Personal narratives were collected from all students three times per year in Grades 3–5, using an open-ended writers workshop approach typical of many elementary classrooms. Because of the large number of waves of writing samples (nine per language), only the results from end-of-year samples for each grade level are presented here.

Finally, the reading measures used a multiple-choice cloze format, in which 30 words were deleted at regular intervals from an otherwise continuous grade-level text and replaced with blanks. Students were asked to choose the most appropriate alternative from among three choices to fill in each blank. One point was awarded for each correct response, with a total possible score of 30 points. English and Spanish cloze reading assessments were administered to all students at the beginning of third grade. However, only an English assessment was administered at the end of fifth grade because of the lack of an available parallel passage for the Spanish assessment. For more information on the measures and findings from this study, see *The Development of Bilingualism and Biliteracy From Grades 3 to 5: A Summary of Findings From the CAL/CREDE Study of Two-Way Immersion Education* (Howard, Christian, et al., 2003).

Because the measures used for the CREDE study are not standardized, the mean performance of native English speakers and native Spanish speakers at each school is compared to that of all native English speakers or all native Spanish speakers in the study at each grade level. To keep these study-wide native language comparison groups consistent for each school, the data for all schools were included in the computations. The benefit of doing this is that the benchmark is consistent across programs; however, the drawback is that it makes it impossible to determine if the performance of students at a given school is significantly different from that of all students in the same native language group in the study as a whole, as one group is a subset of the other. However, as will become evident in the presentation of findings, mean scores at the profiled schools are typically as high as or higher than study means, so the inability to run statistical tests is of limited concern.

Spelling study findings are based on subcomponents of the *Woodcock Language Proficiency Battery, Revised (WLPB-R)*, which has parallel versions in English (Woodcock, 1991) and Spanish (Woodcock & Muñoz-Sandoval, 1991). Specifically, the scores from the English and Spanish picture vocabulary subtest, the broad reading cluster, and the writing skills cluster are provided here as indicators of oral language, reading, and writing ability, respectively. In the findings, we report standard scores, which are based on a standard distribution with a mean of 100 points, a range of 0 to 200 points, and a standard deviation of 15 points. The child's birth date and the date the assessment was administered are both taken into consideration when computing standard scores; thus, standard scores are scale scores, constructed so that average performance of children of the same age is 100 points. Unlike raw scores, which would be expected to increase each year as students' abilities continue to develop over time, standard scores frequently remain fairly stable (or even decrease) from year to year due to the age-group benchmarking that is inherent in the scoring. This does not mean that students are not making progress from year to year; on the contrary, mean scores that remain the same from year to year indicate a full year's progress, and scores that increase from year to year indicate more than a year's worth of progress relative to the norming population. Scores that decline from year to year indicate that students are not making as much progress as the norming population, although they still may be making at least some progress from the previous year. Because the *WLPB-R* is standardized, it is possible to reference the performance of the focal program (in this case, Key) relative to both *WLPB-R* average age-group performance (i.e., 100 points) and mean study-wide findings for all TWI students, both native English speakers and native Spanish speakers. When considering *WLPB-R* mean age-group performance, it is important to point out that the students involved in the calibration group for the Spanish assessments were Spanish monolinguals, most of whom lived in Latin America or Spain; a smaller number were recent arrivals to the United States. As a result, the Spanish norms are questionable for students who have lived all or most of their life in the United States, particularly the native English speakers. However, given the lack of any preferable standardized test in Spanish, these norms at least provide some benchmark for Spanish performance.

For the longitudinal data, descriptive statistics (sample sizes, means, and standard deviations) are presented for each native language group within each school and for all students in the study. In all tables of longitudinal data, n indicates number of students, m indicates mean score, and sd indicates standard deviation. Mean scores for each school are presented in bold if they are as high as or higher than study averages for a given native language group. As discussed earlier, it was not possible to run statistical tests to determine potential statistically significant mean differences between a given school sample and the sample for the study as a whole because the former is a subset of the latter. The frequently small sample sizes in each native language group within each school also presented a methodological obstacle to statistical analysis because of the limited power inherent in small samples, and the subsequent likelihood of failing to find an effect even if it exists. As a result, findings in this book are discussed descriptively. Any differences noted between native language groups within a school or within a native language group between a school and the larger study it participated in should not be interpreted as being statistically significant. The one exception to this is Key, where sample sizes within each native language group were consistently large enough to warrant the use of statistical tests (ANOVA) to look for mean differences across native language groups at each grade level.

As shown in the tables of descriptive statistics, there was student attrition over time at all schools, an anticipated outcome in any longitudinal study. We monitored the cause of each student's departure, and in the clear majority of cases in both studies, moving out of the area was the primary factor (59% in the CREDE study and 67% in the spelling study). Much smaller percentages of students left their respective programs to transfer to a mainstream program, private school, or home schooling (19% in the CREDE study and 24% in the spelling study); transfer to another TWI program (0% in the CREDE study and 3% in the spelling study); academic difficulty resulting in retention or transfer to a special education program (12% in the CREDE study and 6% in the spelling study); or undisclosed reasons (10% in the CREDE study and 0% in the spelling study). For each study, a comparative analysis of students who left versus students who stayed indicated no major differences in background characteristics, meaning that findings over time are not likely to be influenced by a "creaming effect" (i.e., losing a high percentage of special needs students or low-income students) or the reverse.

In addition to the longitudinal data for all schools, there are comparison data in the domains of reading and writing, most of which are based on standardized achievement tests. In some cases, these comparative findings indicate the performance of students in the program relative to state and/or district performance. In other cases, similar data from students in non-TWI programs in the same district are compared to those of TWI students in one of the focal programs.

Overall, the clear message from the findings presented here is that these four programs are very strong. Both native English speakers and native Spanish speakers generally performed well on a variety of measures of language and literacy development in both English and Spanish—relative to other TWI students, to peers in other programs in the district or state, and to test norms. Moreover, in many cases, the performance gap between native English speakers and native Spanish speakers within each program was not as large as is often the case in TWI programs (Howard, Sugarman, et al., 2003). This indicates greater-than-average success in promoting comparable performance for each of the two native language groups within the program. As we noted in the first chapter, not every finding for each of these four schools is exemplary, and there are areas where each school may still be in need of improvement. However, overall, each one of these schools is effective at promoting strong language and literacy outcomes for both native English speakers and native Spanish speakers. Moreover, all of these programs are dedicated to ongoing self-evaluation, reflection, and improvement to address areas in need of improvement. This, in addition to their evident success, contributes to their status as exemplary programs.

Oral Language Development

Longitudinal Findings

Alicia Chacón

On average, both native English speakers (NES) and native Spanish speakers (NSS) at Alicia Chacón demonstrated oral English fluency by the end of fifth grade (Table 3.1). The mean score of NES was slightly higher than that of NSS in third grade, but the mean scores of the two groups were the same at the end of fifth grade. Compared to all students in the study, Alicia Chacón NES scored similarly on average to all NES in the study at both time points, while Alicia Chacón NSS scored slightly lower than all NSS in third grade, but at the same level as all NSS at the end of fifth grade. In Spanish, Alicia Chacón NSS scored slightly higher than Alicia Chacón NES on average in both third and fifth grade, although the gap narrowed to a mere 0.2 points by the end of fifth grade. Both groups scored higher on average than their respective peer groups in the study as a whole in both third and fifth grades, with slightly higher scores for Alicia Chacón NSS (as compared to all NSS in the study) and substantially higher scores for Alicia Chacón NES (as compared to all NES in the study).

Barbieri

As was the case with Alicia Chacón students, on average, both NES and NSS at Barbieri demonstrated oral English fluency by the end of fifth grade (Table 3.1). The mean score of NES was slightly higher than that of NSS in third grade, but the mean scores of the two native language groups were the same at the end of fifth grade. Compared to all students in the study, the average performance in English of both NES and NSS at Barbieri was slightly higher than the respective study averages for their native language peer groups in third grade, and equal to study averages in fifth grade. In Spanish, Barbieri NSS scored higher than NES on average in both third and fifth grades, although the gap was substantially reduced over time. The average scores of Barbieri NSS were at or slightly above the study average for all NSS in both third and fifth grades. The average score in Spanish of Barbieri NES was considerably below the study average for all NES in third grade but within range of the study average by fifth grade.

IAMS

With regard to oral English proficiency, IAMS students demonstrated the same pattern as their peers at Barbieri and Alicia Chacón (Table 3.1). On average, both NES and NSS at IAMS demonstrated oral English fluency by the end of fifth grade. The mean score of NES was slightly higher than that of NSS in third grade, but the mean scores of the two native language groups were the same at the end of fifth grade. Compared to all students in the study, the average performance of both NES and NSS at IAMS was as high as or higher than the respective study averages for their native language peer groups in third grade and fifth grade. In Spanish, NSS at IAMS scored higher on average than NES in both third and fifth grades, although the performance gap between the two groups diminished considerably over time. The average scores in Spanish of NSS at IAMS were slightly above the study average for all NSS in both third and fifth grades. The average score of NES at IAMS was considerably below the study average for all NES in third grade but equal to the study average in fifth grade.

Table 3.1: Summary of Oral Proficiency Findings from the CREDE Study (Scale of 0 to 5 points)

School	Native Language Group	Grade 3			Grade 5		
		n	m	sd	n	m	sd
ENGLISH OUTCOMES							
Alicia Chacón	NSS	22	4.2	0.6	15	**4.9**	0.0
	NES	26	**4.7**	0.1	21	**4.9**	0.1
Barbieri	NSS	12	**4.5**	0.2	12	**4.9**	0.0
	NES	12	**4.8**	0.1	10	**4.9**	0.0
IAMS	NSS	14	**4.6**	0.2	12	**4.9**	0.0
	NES	14	**4.7**	0.2	7	**4.9**	0.0
All students in study	NSS	173	4.3	0.6	124	4.9	0.1
	NES	177	4.7	0.1	117	4.9	0.1
SPANISH OUTCOMES							
Alicia Chacón	NSS	22	**4.7**	0.1	16	**4.9**	0.1
	NES	26	**4.4**	0.4	21	**4.7**	0.1
Barbieri	NSS	12	**4.6**	0.2	12	**4.9**	0.1
	NES	12	1.6	0.6	10	3.8	0.1
IAMS	NSS	13	**4.7**	0.3	12	**4.9**	0.1
	NES	13	2.9	0.9	7	**4.1**	0.8
All students in study	NSS	174	4.6	0.4	125	4.8	0.2
	NES	179	3.5	1.0	116	4.1	0.8

Key

On average, Key NES scored significantly higher than Key NSS on the *WLPB-R* English picture vocabulary subtest in Grades 2–5 ($p < .001$ at all grade levels) (Table 3.2). However, by third grade, mean scores for Key NSS were consistently within one standard deviation of the *WLPB-R* mean age-group performance of 100 points, and mean scores for Key NES were a standard deviation or more above this target. In addition, mean oral English vocabulary scores for both NES and NSS at Key were consistently higher than mean scores for NES and NSS in the study as a whole. In Spanish, on average, Key NES scored significantly lower than Key NSS in Grades 2–5 ($p < .001$ at all grade levels). Mean scores for Key NSS and Key NES were well below *WLPB-R* mean age-group performance (relative to the *WLPB-R* calibration group), with mean scores of Key NES at particularly low levels. This is likely due in part to the calibration sample that was used for the Spanish assessments, namely, Spanish monolingual students predominantly in Latin America and Spain. Moreover, mean oral Spanish vocabulary scores for both NES and NSS at Key were consistently lower than mean scores for NES and NSS in the study as a whole. This suggests that the 50/50 program model is another likely factor in the lower Spanish scores of Key students, as the majority of remaining students in the spelling study were enrolled in 90/10 programs. A recent internal evaluation conducted by the district (Forbes-Ullrich & Perdomo, 2005) also identified oral Spanish proficiency, and vocabulary development in particular, to be a priority area for improvement, and an intervention is currently being designed to address this.

Table 3.2: Summary of Oral Proficiency Findings from the Spelling Study (Scale of 0 to 200 Points)

School	L1	Grade 2			Grade 3			Grade 4			Grade 5		
		n	m	sd	n	m	sd	n	m	sd	n	m	sd
ENGLISH OUTCOMES													
Key	NSS	36	**83.1**	16.77	35	**88.9**	13.80	28	**93.3**	16.57	28	**87.2**	10.37
	NES	39	**118.4**	15.83	36	**118.2**	15.94	32	**114.2**	19.67	28	**117.6**	17.93
All TWI students in study	NSS	118	71.8	21.89	107	78.2	18.71	91	82.9	18.37	83	82.7	13.99
	NES	91	105.8	19.33	81	109.2	17.18	74	104.9	18.49	69	105.6	17.23
SPANISH OUTCOMES													
Key	NSS	36	72.3	22.70	35	76.0	24.85	28	76.0	22.64	29	77.7	24.45
	NES	37	38.7	21.77	36	43.6	24.68	32	37.3	24.29	28	44.5	25.23
All TWI students in study	NSS	123	86.2	24.92	107	84.3	24.53	91	83.8	22.25	83	83.3	23.18
	NES	92	49.0	23.07	81	50.1	25.90	74	48.2	25.39	69	54.0	23.02

Note. Scale scores that remain the same from year to year indicate a full year's progress. For the norming population, *m*=100, *sd*=15.

Discussion

The oral English proficiency outcomes of students at the three schools involved in the CREDE study were remarkably consistent. First, both native Spanish speakers and native English speakers at all schools demonstrated growth in oral English proficiency over time, with both groups achieving fluency by the end of fifth grade. Key School outcomes, while using a different measure, were remarkably similar, as both native language groups again demonstrated growth over time and demonstrated oral English fluency (as defined by mean performance on par with age-group norms) as early as third grade. Other studies have found similar results of oral English fluency among both native English speakers and native Spanish speakers in TWI programs by the upper elementary grades (Howard & Christian, 1997; Howard, Christian, et al., 2003; Lindholm-Leary, 2001; Thomas & Collier, 2002). A recent synthesis of research on the oral language development of English language learners found the same result of advanced oral English proficiency by fifth grade across program types (Saunders & O'Brien, 2006).

Comparing the oral English scores of the two native language groups within each school in the CREDE study, native English speakers had slightly higher scores than native Spanish speakers in third grade, but there was no difference in scores between the two groups by the end of fifth grade. Moreover, with the exception of Alicia Chacón's native Spanish speakers in third grade, both groups of students at all three schools scored as high as or higher than the mean performance of the same native language groups in the study overall. At Key, the mean scores of native English speakers were significantly higher than those of native Spanish speakers at all four grade levels; but with the exception of native Spanish speakers in second grade, both groups consistently demonstrated mean performance on par with age-group norms. Moreover, both native language groups scored above the mean performance of their respective native language groups in the study as a whole at all four grade levels. Other studies on this topic have produced equivocal findings: Some studies reported no significant differences in oral English proficiency across native language groups by Grade 3 (Howard & Christian, 1997) or Grade 5 (Howard, Christian, et al., 2003), and others reported significant differences through Grade 3 (Cazabon et al., 1993).

In Spanish, the oral proficiency outcomes varied more across the schools in the CREDE study, although both native language groups in all three schools showed growth over time and achieved either advanced Spanish proficiency (all native Spanish speakers and native English speakers at Alicia Chacón and IAMS) or high-intermediate levels of Spanish proficiency (Barbieri native English speakers) by the end of fifth grade. Other research has found similar results of growth over time and attainment of advanced levels of Spanish proficiency by the upper elementary grades (Howard, Christian, et al., 2003; Lindholm-Leary, 2001). At Key, both native language groups likewise showed progress in Spanish, but not as much, and attained lower final outcomes by the end of fifth grade. Specifically, on average, both groups of students at Key scored below the mean age-group performance of 100 points in Spanish at all four grade levels, with native English speakers scoring well below this target. This is likely related to a number of factors. First, as was discussed in the introduction to this chapter, there are some questions about whether or not the norms for the Spanish *WLPB-R* are appropriate for bilinguals in the United States, particularly for native English speakers. Second, Key uses a 50/50 program model, and previous research has found that students in 50/50 programs tend to achieve lower levels of Spanish proficiency than students in Spanish-dominant models (Lindholm-Leary, 2001; Lindholm-Leary & Howard, in press). Third, as will be discussed in chapter 8, the school and district are currently undergoing demographic changes, and fewer than half of the current students are native Spanish speakers. This likely creates a greater challenge for the program in trying to promote high levels of Spanish language proficiency for all students.

Previous research has found persistent differences in Spanish oral proficiency attainment between native Spanish speakers and native English speakers in TWI programs (Cazabon et al., 1993; Howard & Christian, 1997; Howard, Christian, et al., 2003). The findings from our focal schools lend further support to these results. At the three schools in the CREDE study, native Spanish speakers consistently performed at higher levels of Spanish proficiency on average than native English speakers, although the gaps between the two groups diminished considerably over time. Relative to whole-study means, native Spanish speakers at all three schools had mean performance in Spanish that was as high as or higher than that of their peers in the study as a whole in both Grades 3 and 5. Native English speakers at Alicia Chacón performed as well as or better than their NES peers in the study as a whole at both grade levels, while native English speakers at Barbieri and IAMS had mean performance that was below the native English speakers study mean in third grade, but comparable to it by the end of fifth grade. This early delay in Spanish proficiency among these two groups of students may be related at least in part to the program model, as both programs provide initial literacy instruction to native English speakers in English only. At Key, the native Spanish speakers performed significantly higher in Spanish than native English speakers at all four grades, and the gap remained consistent over time. In addition, both groups at Key performed below their respective study averages, lending further support to the notion of a potential program model effect, as the majority of other TWI students in the spelling study were enrolled in 90/10 programs.

Reading Development

Longitudinal Findings

Alicia Chacón

On average, both NSS and NES at Alicia Chacón demonstrated growth in English reading ability from the beginning of third grade through the end of fifth grade, with both groups performing at high levels by the end of fifth grade (Table 3.3). NES scored slightly higher than NSS on the English cloze reading assessment in both third and fifth grades. However, the average English cloze reading assessment scores of NSS at Alicia Chacón were higher than the average English cloze reading assessment scores of all NSS in the study in both third grade and fifth grade, indicating comparable performance to their peers in the study as a whole. The average English cloze reading assessment scores of NES at Alicia Chacón were generally comparable to those of all NES in the study as a whole, with a slightly lower mean score in third grade and a slightly higher mean score in fifth grade. The average scores of the two native language groups at Alicia Chacón were comparable on the third grade Spanish cloze reading assessment (the only year it was administered), with both groups posting moderately high scores. In addition, mean scores of both groups were higher than the mean scores of their respective native language peer groups in the study as a whole.

Barbieri

Like Alicia Chacón students, both NSS and NES at Barbieri showed growth in English reading ability, with very high mean scores by the end of fifth grade (Table 3.3). On average, NES at Barbieri scored higher than NSS on the English cloze reading assessment in third grade, but the gap was effectively closed by fifth grade. In addition, the average English cloze reading assessment scores of Barbieri NSS were higher than the average English cloze reading assessment scores of all NSS in the study in both third grade and fifth grade. The average English cloze reading assessment score of Barbieri NES was higher than the average English cloze reading assessment score of all NES in the study in third grade and comparable to the study average in fifth grade. In Spanish, the average score of Barbieri NSS was higher than that of Barbieri NES in third grade. The mean score of Barbieri NSS was also higher than the mean score for all NSS in the study, whereas the mean score of Barbieri NES was lower than the mean score for all NES in the study. However, given that by fifth grade, Barbieri NES achieved parity with their native language peers in the study as a whole on Spanish measures of oral language and writing, it seems likely that this outcome is a function of the differentiated program model. Had the Spanish reading assessment been administered in fifth grade, Barbieri NES would likely have seen scores comparable to those of their native language reference group.

IAMS

Like their counterparts at Alicia Chacón and Barbieri, both NSS and NES at IAMS showed growth in English reading ability from third grade to fifth grade, and both groups had high mean scores by the end of fifth grade (Table 3.3). On average, NES and NSS at IAMS had comparable scores on the English cloze reading assessment in third and fifth grades. In addition, the average English cloze reading assessment scores of NSS and NES were as high as or higher than those of their respective native language peer groups in the study as a whole in both third grade and fifth grade. In Spanish, the average score of NSS was higher than that of NES in third grade. The mean scores of both NSS and NES at IAMS were higher than those of their respective native language peer groups in the study as a whole.

Table 3.3: Summary of Reading Findings from the CREDE Study (Scale of 0 to 30 Points)

School	Native Language Group	Grade 3			Grade 5		
		n	m	sd	n	m	sd
ENGLISH OUTCOMES							
Alicia Chacón	NSS	23	**19.4**	8.6	20	**27.0**	3.8
	NES	26	21.3	5.6	23	**29.0**	1.1
Barbieri	NSS	14	**23.2**	5.5	14	**28.4**	1.3
	NES	25	**27.6**	3.2	23	**29.2**	1.6
IAMS	NSS	24	**23.4**	5.4	22	**27.5**	3.2
	NES	25	**23.7**	6.0	17	28.4	3.2
All students in study	NSS	225	18.1	7.9	177	25.8	4.8
	NES	237	22.7	7.3	167	28.7	2.5
SPANISH OUTCOMES							
Alicia Chacón	NSS	23	**21.7**	7.8			
	NES	26	**21.6**	6.4			
Barbieri	NSS	14	**25.3**	4.4			
	NES	26	14.8	4.9			
IAMS	NSS	23	**25.8**	4.8			
	NES	25	**20.0**	6.0			
All students in study	NSS	221	20.3	7.2			
	NES	238	18.9	6.0			

Key

Looking across native language groups in the school, on average, Key NES scored significantly higher than Key NSS on the English broad reading cluster in Grades 2–5 ($p<.001$ at all four grades) (Table 3.4). However, mean scores for both NES and NSS at Key were consistently as high as or higher than mean scores for NES and NSS in the study as a whole. Moreover, at all four grade levels, on average, both NES and NSS at Key performed at or above the *WLPB-R* age-group mean, and Key NES performed more than a standard deviation above this target. Data from an Arlington Public Schools (APS) immersion program evaluation conducted in part by CAL suggest that this study sample performed very similarly to the district cohorts assessed in the third and fifth grades (Forbes-Ullrich & Perdomo, 2005). In Spanish, Key NSS performed significantly higher on average than Key NES on the broad reading cluster in Grades 2–5 (p<.05 at all four grades). In addition, as was the case with the oral language measure, mean scores for both NES and NSS at Key were consistently lower than mean scores for NES and NSS in the study as a whole, although the differences in this domain were not as great as they were in the domain of oral language. Once again, this is probably indicative at least in part of a program model effect, as the majority of other TWI students in the spelling study were enrolled in 90/10 programs. However, at all four grade levels, both NSS and NES at Key had mean scores that were within one standard deviation or higher of *WLPB-R* mean age-group performance. This is quite remarkable, given that grade-level norms are based primarily on the performance of native Spanish speakers in Latin America and Spain. APS evaluation data suggest that this study sample performed very similarly to the district cohorts assessed in the third and fifth grades (Forbes-Ullrich & Perdomo, 2005).

Table 3.4: Summary of Reading Findings from the Spelling Study (Scale of 0 to 200 Points)

School	L1	Grade 2			Grade 3			Grade 4			Grade 5		
		n	m	sd	n	m	sd	n	m	sd	n	m	sd
ENGLISH OUTCOMES													
Key	NSS	36	**110.3**	13.09	35	**106.7**	12.24	28	**111.3**	13.16	28	**101.9**	10.02
	NES	39	**125.0**	13.89	36	**121.1**	14.96	32	**121.4**	14.09	28	**123.1**	14.76
All TWI students in study	NSS	118	101.3	16.28	107	101.0	12.54	91	103.1	13.97	83	100.2	11.14
	NES	91	114.5	17.06	81	114.3	14.02	74	113.4	14.44	69	115.0	14.95
SPANISH OUTCOMES													
Key	NSS	36	105.2	13.94	35	103.0	11.77	28	101.9	12.01	29	97.0	12.08
	NES	38	96.1	14.65	36	95.9	10.78	32	94.1	11.04	28	89.4	12.31
All TWI students in study	NSS	123	111.1	14.98	107	108.4	13.74	91	105.8	14.31	83	102.1	13.32
	NES	91	103.4	13.54	81	103.2	25.90	74	100.5	11.53	69	94.7	11.25

Note. Scale scores that remain the same from year to year indicate a full year's progress. For the norming population, *m*=100, *sd*=15.

Comparison Group Findings

Alicia Chacón

Comparison findings from the state achievement test (*Texas Assessment of Academic Skills [TAAS]*) that was administered when the students were in fifth grade are very favorable (Table 3.5). A higher percentage of Alicia Chacón students met or exceeded expectations for reading than was the case for either the district or the state.

Table 3.5: Performance of Alicia Chacón Fifth Grade (Spring 2000) Students Relative to State and District Performance in Reading

	% met expectations for reading
State	87
District	91
Alicia Chacón	**97**

In addition, through our own analysis of *TAAS* scores of Alicia Chacón students and students in three comparison monolingual English schools in the district, Alicia Chacón students scored comparably to their native-English-speaking and native-Spanish-speaking peers on standardized reading tests in Spanish or English in Grades 3, 4, and 5 (Table 3.6).

Table 3.6: Reading Performance of Alicia Chacón Students Relative to Performance of District Peers

	Grade 3	Grade 4	Grade 5
Alicia Chacón NSS compared to similar Ysleta NSS	Spanish reading ⇔	Spanish reading ⇔	English reading ⇔
Alicia Chacón NES compared to similar Ysleta NES	English reading ⇔	English reading ⇔	English reading ⇔

Note. ⇔ indicates no statistically significant difference in the performance of the two groups.

IAMS

Comparison findings from the state achievement test (*Illinois Goal Assessment Program [IGAP]*) that was administered when the students were in third grade are very positive (Table 3.7), as a higher percentage of IAMS students met or exceeded district and state performance in reading. This is particularly interesting given that IAMS had higher percentages of language minority students, racial/ethnic minority students, and low-income students than the state, and a higher percentage of language minority students and a comparable percentage of racial/ethnic minority students as the district.

Table 3.7: Performance of IAMS Third Grade (Spring 1998) Students Relative to State and District Performance in Reading

	% met expectations for reading
State	72
District	45
IAMS	**87**

Key

Comparison findings from the state achievement test (*Standards of Learning [SOL]*) that was administered when the students were in fifth grade are once again favorable (Table 3.8), as a higher percentage of Key students passed the state reading test than the average for the district or the state.

Table 3.8: Performance of Key Fifth Grade Students (Spring 2005) Relative to State and District Performance in Reading

	Adjusted passing rate (%) for reading
State	85.0
District	90.3
Key	**96.9**

Barbieri

Comparison data from Barbieri are not available.

Discussion

The English reading outcomes of students at the three schools involved in the CREDE study were remarkably consistent. First, both NSS and NES at all schools demonstrated growth in English reading ability over time, with both groups achieving high mean scores by the end of fifth grade. Key School outcomes, while using a different measure, were remarkably similar, as both native language groups again demonstrated growth over time and demonstrated mean performance higher than the mean *WLPB-R* age-group performance (100 points) at all four grade levels. Other studies have found similar results of strong English reading ability among both NES and NSS in TWI programs by the upper elementary grades (Howard, Christian, et al., 2003; Lindholm-Leary, 2001; Pérez, 2004; Thomas & Collier, 1997, 2002).

Comparing the two native language groups within each school in the CREDE study, NES had slightly higher scores than NSS in third grade at Alicia Chacón and Barbieri, while scores across the two native language groups were comparable at IAMS. At all three schools, by the end of fifth grade, any differences in scores between the two groups were negligible. Moreover, with the exception of Alicia Chacón NSS in third grade and IAMS NES in fifth grade, both groups of students at all three schools scored as high as or higher than the mean performance of the same native language groups in the study overall. At Key, mean scores for NES were significantly higher than those of NSS at all four grade levels, but both groups consistently demonstrated performance above the *WLPB-R* age-group mean. Moreover, both native language groups scored above the mean performance of their respective native language groups in the study as a whole at all four grade levels. Other studies have found significant differences in English reading outcomes between native speakers and second language learners, particularly in the earlier elementary grades (Howard, Christian, et al., 2003; Pérez, 2004).

In Spanish, the reading measure was administered only in third grade, and outcomes varied more across the schools in the CREDE study. With the exception of Barbieri NES, both NSS and NES at all three schools had mean performance that was higher than that of their native language peers in the study as a whole. Within each school, patterns varied somewhat, as NSS and NES at Alicia Chacón had comparable mean scores, while the mean scores of NSS at Barbieri and IAMS were clearly higher than those of NES. At Key, four full waves of Spanish reading data were collected, and the results are impressive. Both native language groups showed progress over time; and although mean scores of both groups were consistently lower than those for all TWI students in the study, they were always within one standard deviation or higher of the *WLPB-R* age-group mean of 100 points at all four grade levels. This is particularly impressive given that the students in the *WLPB-R* calibration sample were Spanish monolinguals residing primarily in Latin America and Spain. At all four grades, the mean score of Key NES was significantly higher than that of Key NSS; but both groups consistently performed within range of the *WLPB-R* age-group score. Previous research has found differences in Spanish reading ability between NSS and NES in TWI programs (Bae & Bachman, 1998; Howard, Christian, et al., 2003; Pérez, 2004).

Looking at the performance of TWI students in our four focal programs relative to that of comparison students in other types of programs within the same districts, or to state and district outcomes, we found very positive results. In all cases, the results for TWI students were as good as or better than those for comparison students or district and state outcomes, and this was the case regardless of the language of assessment. These findings mirror those from large-scale studies that have found that on average, TWI students perform on grade level or higher on standardized reading assessments by the upper elementary grades (Lindholm-Leary, 2001; Thomas & Collier, 1997, 2002).

Writing Development

Longitudinal Findings

Alicia Chacón

Both NSS and NES at Alicia Chacón demonstrated considerable growth in English narrative writing ability from the end of third grade through the end of fifth grade (Table 3.9). Although the average English writing scores of NES at Alicia Chacón started off higher than the average English writing scores of NSS, the gap became progressively smaller over the 3 years of the study. In addition, with the exception of NSS in third grade, the average English writing scores of both NES and NSS at Alicia Chacón were consistently as high as or higher than the mean scores of their respective native language groups in the study as a whole. Moreover, by fifth grade, the average English writing score of Alicia Chacón NSS was the same as the average English writing score of all NES in the study.

In Spanish, both language groups demonstrated growth over the 3 years of the study. Although the average Spanish writing scores of NSS at Alicia Chacón were higher than the average Spanish writing scores of NES, the gap was always very slight. As was the case with English writing, at all three time points, the average Spanish writing scores of both NSS and NES at Alicia Chacón were higher than study averages for their respective groups. Moreover, by fifth grade, the average Spanish writing scores of NES at Alicia Chacón were comparable to the average Spanish writing scores for all NSS in the study. In other words, in both their first and second language writing ability, both NES and NSS at Alicia Chacón achieved parity with study averages for native speakers by the end of fifth grade.

Barbieri

Like their peers at Alicia Chacón, both NSS and NES at Barbieri made considerable progress in English writing ability from third through fifth grade (Table 3.9). But at Barbieri, the average English writing scores of NES were consistently higher than the average English writing scores of NSS, with the gap remaining fairly consistent over time. In addition, average English writing scores of both NES and NSS at Barbieri were consistently as high as or higher than the mean scores of their respective native language groups in the study as a whole. Moreover, the average English writing scores of Barbieri NSS were consistently comparable to the average English writing scores of all NES in the study.

In Spanish, both language groups demonstrated considerable progress over time, particularly the NES, who started off quite low in third grade. While the average Spanish writing scores of Barbieri NSS were consistently higher than those of Barbieri NES, the gap narrowed considerably over time. The average Spanish writing scores of Barbieri NSS were consistently higher than NSS study averages. Although Barbieri NES average scores in Spanish writing were well below the study average in third grade, they showed dramatic improvement over the 3 years of the study, with average scores in fifth grade that were comparable to study averages for both NES and NSS.

IAMS

Both NSS and NES at IAMS demonstrated mean growth in English writing ability from third grade through fifth grade, but not quite as much as the students at Alicia Chacón or Barbieri or in the study as a whole (Table 3.9). The average English writing scores of NES and NSS at IAMS were comparable at all three grades, with only slight differences favoring NES. In addition, average English writing scores of NSS at IAMS were consistently higher than the mean scores of all NSS in the study as a whole, and average English writing scores of NES at IAMS were comparable to but slightly lower than mean scores for all NES in the study.

In Spanish, both language groups demonstrated mean progress in writing ability. Although the average Spanish writing scores of NSS at IAMS were consistently higher than those of NES, the gap was generally very slight. The average Spanish writing scores of NSS at IAMS were consistently higher than NSS study averages, and the performance of NES at IAMS was higher than or comparable to the mean performance of all NES in the study.

Table 3.9: Summary of Writing Findings from the CREDE Study (Scale of 0 to 5 Points)

School	Native Language Group	Grade 3			Grade 4			Grade 5		
		n	m	sd	n	m	sd	n	m	sd
ENGLISH OUTCOMES										
Alicia Chacón	NSS	21	2.6	1.0	20	**3.6**	0.5	17	**4.0**	0.6
	NES	24	**3.4**	0.8	24	**4.0**	0.4	23	**4.2**	0.5
Barbieri	NSS	14	**3.2**	0.6	13	**3.7**	0.4	14	**4.0**	0.4
	NES	27	**3.6**	0.6	24	**4.2**	0.4	22	**4.5**	0.3
IAMS	NSS	24	**3.4**	0.3	21	**3.7**	0.4	20	**3.9**	0.4
	NES	25	**3.5**	0.4	16	3.9	0.5	16	4.0	1.1
All students in study	NSS	217	2.8	0.8	194	3.5	0.7	170	3.8	0.6
	NES	234	3.3	0.7	183	4.0	0.6	167	4.2	0.7
SPANISH OUTCOMES										
Alicia Chacón	NSS	24	**3.1**	0.9	20	**3.9**	0.6	15	**4.1**	0.5
	NES	27	**3.0**	0.7	22	**3.7**	0.5	22	**3.9**	0.6
Barbieri	NSS	14	**3.5**	0.6	14	**3.9**	0.5	14	**4.1**	0.4
	NES	23	1.9	0.9	25	3.0	0.7	23	3.5	0.3
IAMS	NSS	23	**3.3**	0.5	21	**3.5**	0.5	21	**4.0**	0.5
	NES	25	**3.1**	0.5	16	3.1	0.4	14	**3.8**	0.6
All students in study	NSS	213	2.9	0.8	202	3.4	0.7	165	3.8	0.7
	NES	232	2.6	0.9	187	3.2	0.8	165	3.7	0.7

Key

On average, the mean English writing skills cluster performance of Key NES was significantly higher than that of Key NSS at all grade levels ($p<.001$ at all four grades) (Table 3.10). However, mean scores for both NES and NSS at Key were consistently as high as or higher than mean scores for NES and NSS in the study as a whole. Moreover, at all four grade levels, on average, both NES and NSS at Key performed within one standard deviation or higher of the *WLPB-R* mean age-group score of 100 points. APS evaluation data suggest that this study sample performed very similarly to the district cohorts assessed in the third and fifth grades (Forbes-Ullrich & Perdomo, 2005). In Spanish, there was no significant difference in mean performance across the two native language groups at any grade level. However, mean Spanish writing scores for both NES and NSS at Key were consistently lower than mean scores for all TWI NES and NSS in the study. Similarly, the mean performance of Key students was only comparable to *WLPB-R* age-group mean performance in Grade 2 for the NES and in Grades 2 and 3 for the NSS. Again, APS evaluation data suggest that this study sample performed very similarly to the district cohorts assessed in the third and fifth grades (Forbes-Ullrich & Perdomo, 2005). As was the case with the oral language outcomes reported earlier, this is probably related to a number of factors, including the student population of the Spanish calibration sample for the assessment (i.e., Spanish monolinguals, primarily in Latin America and Spain), the 50/50 program model, and the decreasing number of native Spanish speakers at Key.

Table 3.10: Summary of Writing Findings from the Spelling Study (Scale of 0 to 200 Points)

School	L1	Grade 2			Grade 3			Grade 4			Grade 5		
		n	m	sd	n	m	sd	n	m	sd	n	m	sd
ENGLISH OUTCOMES													
Key	NSS	36	96.9	13.71	35	94.7	13.23	28	96.3	14.50	28	89.6	12.26
	NES	39	115.2	14.80	36	111.6	15.86	32	109.9	16.88	28	110.7	17.23
All students in study	NSS	118	82.4	19.65	107	87.7	13.23	91	89.6	14.02	83	86.7	11.55
	NES	91	100.1	19.08	81	101.8	15.75	74	101.6	16.03	69	99.8	16.04
SPANISH OUTCOMES													
Key	NSS	36	91.0	12.98	35	86.9	13.47	28	84.9	11.9	29	84.1	14.38
	NES	37	88.0	16.87	36	82.4	10.91	32	81.2	13.17	28	79.3	11.51
All students in study	NSS	123	96.7	13.84	107	91.6	14.38	91	89.6	13.84	83	86.7	12.88
	NES	92	90.5	13.97	81	87.2	10.47	74	85.7	12.31	69	82.8	10.31

Note. Scale scores that remain the same from year to year indicate a full year's progress. For the norming population, $m=100$, $sd=15$.

Comparison Group Findings

Alicia Chacón

Comparison findings from the state achievement test (*TAAS*) that was administered when the students were in fourth grade are very favorable (Table 3.11). A higher percentage of Alicia Chacón students met or exceeded expectations for writing than was the case for either the district or the state.

Table 3.11: Performance of Alicia Chacón Fourth Grade (Spring 1999) Students Relative to State and District Performance In Writing

	% met expectations for English writing	% met expectations for Spanish writing
State	88.4	67.8
District	91.3	84.4
Alicia Chacón	**97.0**	**85.3**

In addition, in our own comparison of *TAAS* scores of Alicia Chacón students with *TAAS* scores of students in three comparison monolingual English schools in the district, Alicia Chacón NSS scored comparably to their native-Spanish-speaking peers on standardized writing tests in Spanish in Grade 4, and Alicia Chacón NES scored significantly higher than their peers in English writing (Table 3.12).

Table 3.12: Fourth Grade Writing Performance of Alicia Chacón Students Relative to District Peers' Performance

	Grade 4
Alicia Chacón NSS compared to similar Ysleta NSS	Spanish writing ⇔
Alicia Chacón NES compared to similar Ysleta NES	English writing ⇑

Note. ⇔ indicates no statistically significant difference in the performance of the two groups, and ⇑ indicates that Alicia Chacón students scored significantly higher than their Ysleta NES peers in monolingual English programs.

Barbieri

The English and Spanish writing performance of Barbieri NSS was compared with that of NSS in the late-exit bilingual program in the same district (Caswell & Howard, 2004). English and Spanish narrative writing samples were collected from students in both programs over a period of several years (Grades 3 through 5) and scored using the measure developed for the CREDE study that was discussed in the introduction to this chapter. Uncontrolled mean findings over time were as follows:

- For both TWI and late-exit students in both languages, means over time were consistently highest in grammar and lowest in composition, with mechanics in between.
- TWI means were higher than late-exit means on all components and overall.

- Over time, mean scores in English composition showed the least differences across program type, while mean scores in Spanish composition showed the greatest differences.
- Patterns of mean scores over time in Spanish and English were similar within each program.

Performance at the end of fifth grade was analyzed using multiple regression. After controlling for socioeconomic status, gender, special education, and country of origin, the following was found:

- No significant differences were found between TWI and late-exit students in end-of-fifth-grade English writing scores, either overall or on any component. Moreover, both groups scored comparably in English to the TWI native English speakers (i.e., no significant differences across groups).
- Significant differences were found in end-of-fifth-grade Spanish writing scores, with TWI students scoring higher in the Spanish overall score and in the composition subscore.

In summary, by the end of fifth grade, English writing performance was comparable among TWI NES, TWI NSS, and late-exit bilingual NSS, while the Spanish writing performance of TWI NSS was significantly higher than that of late-exit bilingual NSS, indicating a TWI program advantage in native language maintenance and the development of biliteracy.

IAMS

Comparison findings from the *IGAP*, the state achievement test that was administered when the students were in third grade, are impressive (Table 3.13), as a higher percentage of IAMS students met or exceeded district and state performance in writing. As discussed in the presentation of similar findings in the reading domain, this is particularly interesting given that IAMS had comparable or higher percentages of language minority students, racial and ethnic minority students, and students who qualified for free or reduced-price lunch.

Table 3.13: Performance of IAMS Third Grade (Spring 1998) Students Relative to State and District Performance

	% met expectations for writing
State	87
District	76
IAMS	**95**

Key

Comparison findings from the state achievement test (*SOL*) that was administered when the students were in fifth grade are impressive across the board (Table 3.14). Students did very well at the state, district, and school levels, with an equally high or higher percentage of Key students passing the state writing test relative to district and state performance.

Table 3.14: Performance of Key Fifth Grade Students (Spring 2005) Relative to State and District Performance

	Adjusted passing rate (%) for writing
State	91.0
District	93.0
Key	**93.2**

Discussion

The English writing outcomes of students at the three schools involved in the CREDE study were fairly consistent. First, both NSS and NES at all schools demonstrated growth in English writing ability over time, although the amount of mean growth varied somewhat across schools. With the exception of Alicia Chacón's NSS in third grade and IAMS' NES in fourth and fifth grades, both NSS and NES at the three schools demonstrated mean performance that was as high as or higher than that of their respective native language groups in the study as a whole. The Key School data, which used a different measure, were similar, as both native language groups again demonstrated growth over time and demonstrated higher mean performance than other TWI students in the study. In addition, at all four grade levels, the mean performance of Key NSS and NES was within one standard deviation or higher of the *WLPB-R* age-group mean of 100 points. Other studies, primarily those involving the full CREDE dataset, have also found growth in English writing ability (Howard, 2003; Howard & Christian, 1997; Howard, Christian, et al., 2003).

Comparing the two native language groups within each school in the CREDE study, NES typically had higher scores than NSS at all three grade levels, but the differences were frequently negligible, particularly by fifth grade. At Key, mean scores for NES were significantly higher than those for NSS at all four grade levels; but both groups consistently demonstrated mean performance within a standard deviation or higher of the *WLPB-R* age-group mean. Related analyses of the full CREDE dataset have found continued significant differences across native language groups, albeit diminishing ones (Howard, 2003; Howard, Christian, et al., 2003).

In Spanish, both NES and NSS at all three schools in the CREDE study likewise showed mean growth over time in their writing ability. The related studies referenced previously have found similar trends of growth in Spanish writing by both NSS and NES in TWI programs (Howard, 2003; Howard & Christian, 1997; Howard, Christian, et al., 2003). With the exception of IAMS' NES in fourth grade and Barbieri's NES at all three grade levels, mean scores of both native language groups were consistently as high as or higher than mean scores for their respective native language groups in the study as a whole. At Key, both native language groups likewise showed mean progress in Spanish writing, but typically not as much as the calibration sample (leading to a decline in standard scores over time); mean scores were consistently lower than those of their TWI peers in the study as a whole. With the exception of NSS in Grades 2 and 3 and NES in Grade 2, the mean Spanish writing performance of Key students was not within the range of the *WLPB-R* age-group mean. As has been discussed previously, this is likely related to factors such as the nature of the assessment, the program model, and the student population at Key.

Persistent differences in Spanish writing ability between NSS and NES in TWI programs have been found in the related research discussed earlier (Howard, 2003; Howard & Christian, 1997; Howard, Christian, et al., 2003). The findings from our focal schools are more equivocal, as differences, when they do exist, tend to be negligible. At the three schools in the CREDE study,

NSS consistently performed at higher levels on average than NES, although the gaps between the two groups were typically minimal, except at Barbieri. At Key, there were no significant differences in mean Spanish writing scores at any grade level.

Looking at the performance of TWI students in our four focal programs relative to that of comparison students in other types of programs within the same districts, or to state and district outcomes, we found very positive results. In all cases, the results for TWI students were as good as or better than those for comparison students or district and state outcomes, regardless of the language of assessment.

Conclusion

A number of conclusions can be drawn from the patterns of findings that are discussed in this chapter and supported by the existing research base in the field.

First, **both native Spanish speakers and native English speakers demonstrated mean growth in language and literacy abilities in both English and Spanish,** providing evidence of continued progress toward the goal of bilingualism and biliteracy development (Howard, Christian, et al., 2003; Lindholm-Leary, 2001).

Second, there seems to be a **native language effect** such that native speakers generally demonstrate higher mean performance than second language speakers in both oral and written language proficiency, although these differences tend to diminish over time and are sometimes negligible (Cazabon et al., 1993; Howard, 2003; Howard, Christian, et al., 2003).

Third, not surprisingly, there seem to be slightly different patterns for native English speakers and native Spanish speakers, with **native English speakers always showing a clear dominance in and preference for English, and native Spanish speakers demonstrating more balanced bilingualism** (Cazabon et al., 1993; Ha, 2001; Howard, 2003; Howard, Christian, et al., 2003). Sometimes the mean performance of native Spanish speakers is slightly higher in their native language and other times slightly higher in English; in general, however, their mean performance on language and literacy measures across languages is much more similar than that of their native-English-speaking peers, who are consistently dominant in English.

Fourth, there is some evidence for a **program model effect.** Less Spanish instruction in the primary grades (i.e., 50/50 model or differentiated model for NES) results in lower Spanish performance at all grade levels. More Spanish instruction in the primary grades (i.e., 90/10 or modified 90/10) sometimes results in lower mean English performance in the primary grades, with comparable mean performance in English by the upper elementary grades (Lindholm-Leary & Howard, in press).

Finally, comparison data indicate that on average, **TWI students tend to perform at levels comparable to or higher than their non-TWI peers in the district and state** (Caswell & Howard, 2004; Howard, 2002; Lindholm-Leary, 2001; Thomas & Collier, 1997, 2002).

Chapter 4:
Promoting Bilingualism and Biliteracy Through a Culture of Intellectualism

Introduction

As we have engaged in dual language research and technical assistance activities over the past decade, we have traveled the country and visited many TWI programs, observing classrooms and talking with teachers, administrators, parents, and students. In so doing, we have been struck by what we have come to call "a culture of intellectualism" in many highly effective programs, such as the four profiled in this book. This, in fact, is what started us thinking about the idea that the use of effective instructional strategies—while undeniably essential for promoting desired student outcomes—seems more effective when employed in a larger context that supports learning, at both the classroom and school levels. Clearly, a key factor in any context that supports learning, that of both the adults and the students in the building, is a culture of intellectualism.

Specifically, our research indicates that this culture of intellectualism is defined by the following four characteristics, each of which will be explored in depth in this chapter through the use of instructional vignettes and quotes from teachers in the four focal programs:

- A commitment to ongoing learning, meaning that there is an atmosphere of reflection and change; an attitude that it's OK to make mistakes; and high expectations for oneself and others

- Collaboration and exchange of ideas through the expression of multiple points of view, the use of multiple approaches to problem solving, and the acceptance of more than one correct answer
- The fostering of independence through the provision of choices, encouragement of self-monitoring and self-motivation, and instruction in problem-solving strategies
- The promotion of higher order thinking skills, such as predicting, analyzing, interpreting, synthesizing, and applying

At the classroom level, other researchers have shown that a similar constellation of features is important for the academic success of both mainstream students (Brown & Campione, 1994) and linguistically and culturally diverse students (Rogoff, Matusov, & White, 1996; Tharp & Gallimore, 1988). At the school level, various elements of what we call intellectualism have been the basis in part for key school reform models, such as Comer's School Development Program and Sizer's Coalition of Essential Schools (Stringfield, Datnow, & Ross, 1998). Likewise, recent pedagogical guidelines developed by research centers stress the need for an intellectual focus in schools (Dalton, 1998; Resnick & Hall, 2005). Finally, in their comprehensive works on the subject, Howley, Howley, and Pendarvis (1995) and Kohn (1999) explore the anti-intellectual forces at work in public education and put forth well-elaborated discussions on the need for a move toward intellectualism in schools today. Building on this body of knowledge, we argue that a culture of intellectualism is an essential feature of effective dual language programs at both the classroom and school levels, with a specific focus on the development of bilingualism and biliteracy.

The following sections offer vignettes and quotes that exemplify a culture of intellectualism. Although each section focuses on one of the four specific defining characteristics listed above, many of the quotes and vignettes demonstrate more than one characteristic of a culture of intellectualism.

Commitment to Ongoing Learning

Reflection and Change

A commonality across the four effective programs involved in our studies is that they all exhibit a commitment to ongoing learning for both adults and children. First, they offer highly reflective environments, where individuals are continually examining how things are working and how things could be changed for the better. A recent review of research and best practices in dual language education cited the need to infuse the idea of reflective practice into professional development activities, thus underscoring the importance of this issue for dual language teachers in particular (Lindholm-Leary, 2005). Minerva Gonzalez, a former second-grade teacher and current principal of Barbieri, summarized her program's philosophy by saying, "I think a program that self-assesses and constantly evaluates is more likely to do well than one that doesn't." Ester de Jong, then assistant director of bilingual education for Framingham (the district where Barbieri is located) elaborated on this idea when she addressed a question regarding who promoted the atmosphere of fluid change:

> Susan [McGilvray, director of bilingual education] and I do that. The teachers themselves do that. They're very reflective teachers, and they want to do the best for the kids. And so one thing that Framingham has started doing very consistently is looking at assessment, and looking at achievement scores, and listening to the feedback that we've gotten from the middle school and the high school ... also from [the Lesley University] literacy initiative ... and thinking about "so what are the implications for our model of that?" And so I think it's a combination of staffing—[teachers being] very reflective and wanting to do things better—and leadership that says, "Yeah, we need to constantly, critically examine what we're doing." And using the feedback that we're getting from parents, from other teachers, and thinking about what we can do, and trying to support it as much as we can through whatever means the system has.

As Ester conveyed in this quote, in highly effective programs, this atmosphere of reflection and change is supported by and participated in by administrators, teachers, and parents working in a mutually supportive fashion.

Similar sentiments were echoed by teachers at Key who participated in the 2-year teacher-research project supported by the Spencer Foundation. The seven teachers developed research skills and carried out independent research projects in their classrooms on topics of interest related to language and literacy development. (See chapter 7 for the project description of one of these teachers, Ivonne Govea.) A first-grade Spanish teacher related her experiences as a teacher-researcher:

> *Haciendo una investigación, nos dio una oportunidad de hacer preguntas si lo que hacíamos estaba en la* [Doing a study gave us the opportunity to question if what we were doing was in the] right direction, or if there was something else we could do better to help the kids. The research would give us the knowledge [and] methods, from observing to analyzing data, and this is very valuable in terms of teaching and all of life, too. Another thing I've found [helpful] has been the interaction with the kids, having a more intimate relationship—and they knew, too, that we were doing a special project with them.... And the third thing has been the results: As we saw them, we saw what we had to cover to improve teaching and the learning process.

This teacher nicely summarized the experiences of the teachers in the group: They were able to reflect on an issue of importance to them related to their students' language and literacy development, they developed the research skills that enabled them to investigate their question, and they obtained results that ultimately served to inform their instruction. This teacher's sentiments were echoed by her colleague, Marleny Perdomo, a fourth-grade Spanish teacher at the time of the study, as she discussed the benefits of participating in the project and investigating her students' understanding of word problems:

> For me, the benefits of participating in teacher research were multiple. Research allowed me to become much more aware of my role as a teacher and taught me to make adjustments to my teaching on the spot in order to meet my students' needs. Doing research on how students learn taught me that the interaction between teacher and students is crucial in the delivery of instruction. I became aware of my choice of words and paid close attention to students' responses, deciding when it was appropriate to change a question or to paraphrase something to make the content clear to my students, or to simply elicit more conversation on the problem at hand. Because teacher research allowed me to look at my teaching more introspectively, it made me reaffirm the importance of my role in the classroom. It made me gain more respect for my profession. Research also made me realize that there are not definitive answers in teaching, and that a good teacher is always looking for ways to do things better.

From Marleny's perspective, becoming a teacher-researcher helped her to reflect not only on her students' learning, but on her teaching as well, and this both informed her practice and gave her greater respect for herself and her chosen profession. Finally, Marleny's research partner, Patricia Martínez, a Spanish special education teacher, described her participation in a similar way:

> I think it just keeps you learning all the time. I was always looking for courses or books. This made me look for a lot of information. And it made me very reflective and pay a lot of attention to what students said.... It changes the way you teach forever. I don't think I could not do it now.

Marleny and Patricia went on to present the findings from their research at the Spencer Practitioner Research and Communication Mentoring grantees' conference. In this way, they helped to convey information about linguistic and cultural diversity and TWI education to a mainstream audience, and they also joined the larger community of teacher-researchers beyond the school walls.

At the classroom level, the reflection and change inherent in ongoing learning is frequently evident in programs that use a lot of project-based learning, such as IAMS and Alicia Chacón. In these programs, students are highly engaged in learning and continue to investigate topics over time, through multiple modalities. They are given opportunities to make predictions, confirm or refute those predictions, and extend their knowledge as a result. The following vignette from a third-grade classroom at IAMS provides a good example of this. This lesson—which promotes higher order thinking, uses thematic instruction, and integrates language and content objectives—was based on the students' ongoing investigation of the Incas. In it, the teacher promotes reflection and allows students to revisit an activity to gain increasingly higher levels of understanding.

> The teacher told the students that she was going to pass back a sheet that they had been working on about the Incas, announcing, "*Algunos faltan información. Hoy vamos a averiguar que todos tienen la misma información. Pueden utilizar los libros. En veinte minutos vamos a repasar toda la información juntos.* [Some of you are missing information. Today we're going to check to make sure that everyone has the same information. You can use your books. In 20 minutes we're going to review everything together.]" She passed out the papers and the books and told everyone that she wanted a list of what the Incas ate

during the day. The sheet that she passed back was a worksheet with questions drawn from the book about what the Incas did. On each student's paper, she had marked a grade with a check system and asked for information that had been missing. The students needed to search in the book for the information that they had missed. Most had missed the bit about what the Incas ate. The teacher went around to help those who needed it. A student who finished early also went around to offer his help to others. At one point, some students who were talking in English were told by their classmates to speak in Spanish. Later, the teacher went over the worksheet with the students, discussing the foods the Incas ate and the engineering feats of the Incas with the entire class, as well as the other information on the worksheet. She drew mountains on the blackboard and talked about the Andes and engineering wonders of the Incas, who were building roads and bridges through the mountains.

On a different day, this same teacher demonstrated an ability to be reflective about her students' moods and to make an immediate change to her instructional plans to incorporate children's experiences and interests into a brief instructional episode.

The students were returning to their room after visiting an exhibit given by another class. In the stairway on their way back, the teacher told the students to take out their Spanish notebooks when they got back to the classroom. But when the students arrived, they were very excited because of the time they had spent in the exhibit and because it was the first day of snow. They all gathered around the window looking at the snow. The teacher turned off the lights and the students got into their chairs. The teacher wrote on the blackboard:

> *Nieve, nieve*
> *dice mi canción*
> *copita de nieve*
> *es mi corazón.*

> [The snow, the snow
> Sings my song
> A snowflake
> Is my heart.]

> She told the students to write the poem in their notebooks and to put the date so that they would know what the first day of snow was. They then read the poem together.

In this way, the teacher was able to capitalize on her students' enthusiasm about the snow, and rather than losing them to the excitement of the weather, found a way to channel their energy back into a related literacy activity that settled them down and prepared them for the rest of the day's instruction.

Finally, Minerva Gonzalez, then a second-grade teacher at Barbieri, discussed how she has changed her instructional practices over the years based on feedback from teachers in the subsequent grade, and also how she succeeded in promoting parent participation in the process:

> Whether they test at my grade level or not, I clearly feel the pressure, like every other teacher, because I understand that education is not just the responsibility of one grade but of all grades. Clearly a lot of my instructional changes throughout the years, especially in two-way, have been in response to the children's performance in third grade. As an example, the students were not accustomed to homework in Spanish when entering third grade, so I began to implement one or two homework assignments per unit to get them ready for that expectation. Students often forgot vocabulary words from one grade to the next. In response to this, in second grade we created Spanish-English journal dictionaries that students could take home at the end of the year. These journal dictionaries contain all the words that the students have learned for every unit in second grade. They serve as resources for parents over the summer, as parents are encouraged to make word banks and activities with the words. When the third-grade teacher was encouraging students to use resources around them, they pulled out their journal dictionaries and asked if they could use them. The third-grade teacher saw their usefulness, and together we made it a requirement for second graders to bring the journal dictionaries to third grade.

Mistakes Are OK

In an environment where there's a commitment to ongoing learning, it's OK to make mistakes, since that is acknowledged to be a normal part of the learning process. At the program level, this attitude was expressed by Minerva Gonzalez of Barbieri:

> I think we all have areas that could use improvement. If we didn't think that way and if we weren't self-assessing, we wouldn't grow. An area I can identify that we can improve on is in the instruction of Spanish grammar for second language learners. We need to more effectively integrate grammar instruction into our content instruction.

Programs that are not afraid to look critically at themselves, to acknowledge areas where they may not be performing at the level that they would like to, and then put the energy and resources toward remedying that situation are most likely to produce high-level outcomes for students.

Similarly, in programs where teachers see themselves as learners and are willing to expose their vulnerabilities to promote their own learning and, ultimately, improve their instruction, teachers serve as strong role models for students. A teacher at IAMS exemplified this by saying, "For me, especially when I was new, some teachers would speak to me in Spanish and they would correct me sometimes. That really helps a lot, speaking to each other in Spanish." This is a powerful sentiment, as it conveys that the larger school environment is committed to using Spanish beyond the classroom, and that teachers are willing to take risks with the language (and it is safe for them to do so) while they encourage their students to do the same.

The same type of safe atmosphere for making mistakes helps students take risks with their second language at the classroom level. Upper elementary teachers at Alicia Chacón commented on how their students make frequent presentations to their peers, especially in small groups. One teacher commented,

> The new Language to Literacy program is also helpful because there are no wrong answers, so the students feel free to answer anything and not worry about the "correct" answer. Native Spanish speakers see native English speakers taking the risk to speak in Spanish, and so they take the risk to speak in English, and they see that it's OK to make mistakes and no one's there to criticize.... There is a general understanding that mistakes are allowed and that being corrected is OK. The students themselves have instilled this expectation in themselves.

High Expectations

Finally, a commitment to ongoing learning is characterized by high expectations for oneself and others. Among the staff at the four effective programs profiled here, there were clearly high expectations for themselves: The majority had advanced degrees, and many participated in stimulating professional activities such as attending and presenting at conferences, conducting teacher research, and engaging in ongoing discussions about teaching and learning within the program. Marleny Perdomo of Key Elementary talks about her decision to engage in teacher research and how it changed her teaching:

> I had never done any research in the classroom, and I felt that was a new step, something I hadn't tried. I had always reflected on my teaching but never took notes or did any research in the classroom. I had been teaching for 7 years, and I was curious to see what you can find out when you start monitoring your teaching in a more systematic way. In the beginning it seemed very easy. Later, writing and reflecting became overwhelming, because it was hard to articulate all my thoughts (there was so much to say!) and because of time constraints. But when we finished writing [the paper] and we presented at the conference … it just seemed that it was so worth it because I can tell that I'm not the same teacher. I'm looking at the students and wondering what they're thinking and what I can do to help them understand the concept we're studying. This constant reflection that produces change is the greatest benefit I drew from participating in teacher research. I feel like every teaching opportunity is gravitating toward this question that I have in my mind.

In other words, Marleny was ready to try something new that would invigorate her teaching practice and the learning of her students. At first she found the process difficult and overwhelming, but she persevered and ultimately gained a lot of knowledge, skills, and insights from her experiences.

Staff in highly effective TWI programs also have high expectations for their students, of course. This is essential; research on effective programs for linguistically and culturally diverse students has found high expectations to be a crucial component for academic success (Brisk, 2006; Carter & Chatfield, 1986; Lucas, Henze, & Donato, 1990). Middle school teachers at Alicia Chacón related that former students come back to visit them from high school and speak of how easy high school is. Even the high school teachers themselves have told them that the middle school program is covering so much that the students are coming to them more than prepared for high school. The middle school teachers require students to do presentations, research projects, travel modules, and many other activities that combine the three program languages and all subject areas. Their high expectations of students at Alicia Chacón has an impact not only on the students, but also on their subsequent teachers in high school, who are then compelled to provide increasingly challenging material for the students.

At the upper elementary level, as well, Alicia Chacón teachers have high expectations for students. In cases where students in one classroom are at different academic levels, the general rule is to teach to the highest level of academic achievement, allowing the entire class to move up to that level. This approach is supported by research, which has found that effective schools promote the achievement of their struggling students by accelerating instruction rather than by slowing it down (Lindholm-Leary, 2005). Exposing the students to a lot of literature and other print matter is a strategy that Alicia Chacón teachers use, both because there are so many levels of print available and because it is possible to modify print materials to make them accessible to students at a range of levels. Additionally, teachers find that the frequent use of small-group cooperative learning and flexible grouping helps accommodate the students' individual needs.

Collaboration and Exchange of Ideas

A second characteristic central to a culture of intellectualism is frequent collaboration and exchange of ideas, which allows individuals to see that there are multiple points of view, multiple approaches to solving a problem, and, in many cases, more than one appropriate solution. At the program level, this approach most frequently plays out among teachers as they collaborate with each other and share their challenges and successes. This form of teacher collaboration can occur between English/Spanish partners; among grade-level peers; between classroom teachers and resource teachers; among teachers from a variety of grades within the program; and even across sites in cases where district-level programs extend to the high school level, which is true of all of our focal programs except IAMS. A recent review of research and best practices in dual language programs has found these types of collaborative exchanges to be essential for promoting an effective learning environment (Lindholm-Leary, 2005).

Primary teachers at IAMS talked about how they engage in ongoing planning with a grade-level partner to make sure they are staying on track with language goals for their students.

> What we do in group work with our classes, something we do as teachers a lot, we coach each other, we have a partner, we plan together—so all of that really motivates and helps us and helps us fine tune some areas and get ideas in other areas where we're weak and might need some encouragement. We meet every week as teachers, and that makes a big difference, so we can work on those things that we might be slipping up on, as far as the language and what to do with the students to address those issues.

Although this collaboration happens fairly regularly at IAMS, there was a sentiment that it would be helpful to have even more time for teachers to collaborate and be able to share what works and what doesn't. A similar sentiment was expressed by an ESL teacher at Barbieri, who did manage to have informal conversations with classroom teachers and to build on what they were doing in the classroom (such as using Venn diagrams with ESL students in second grade at the same time that the classroom teacher was using them in Spanish). The ESL teacher also received a list of topics and a timeline for their coverage from each teacher at the beginning of the year, but she would have appreciated a more consistent, formal planning time: "I wish we had a time where we could plan more. I mean, I see what's going on in the classroom, but I don't have time to sit down with the teachers.... A third-grade [teacher] will say, 'Well if you're doing that, I'll do this,' but it's not a formalized planning time, so that I'd love to see."

While collaborating with other teachers was generally viewed as a support, teachers acknowledged that it can present challenges as well. Patricia Martínez, a Spanish special education teacher at Key who worked collaboratively as a teacher and co-researcher with Marleny Perdomo in her fourth-grade Spanish classroom, expressed this by saying, "It was very good working with Marleny. In some ways it's more difficult, but it's also a support. It has to be somebody that you really want to work with, someone whose personality is compatible with yours."

The value of collaborating with an external facilitator who does not have an evaluative role was conveyed by Evelyn Fernández, the assistant principal at Key, when reflecting on the success of the teacher-research project at the school:

> Another component that I think was effective was the collaboration aspect, because it counters the isolation of the classroom. Teachers

need mutual support, they need the opportunity to offer feedback to their colleagues and to learn from others' teaching approaches. They also need to have feedback from a facilitator who's not evaluative. It creates a supportive environment and creates a comfort level for them to be able to share personal teaching successes and failures. And it gives them a sense that they can take chances and experiment because others are doing the same.

As Evelyn indicated, the value of this type of approach is that teachers feel safe to disclose their struggles because the facilitator is from outside of the school and does not have an evaluative function. As a result, an environment where teachers take risks and learn from each other is created, thus resulting in more effective professional development and a greater impact on student learning.

Finally, in programs that are articulated to the secondary level, it is possible to have a feedback chain from the secondary to the elementary grades as well as collaboration across teachers from various grade levels. This helps shape program-wide language goals and ensure that all teachers do their part to help students attain those goals. Ester de Jong of Framingham discussed this in the context of Barbieri and its partner programs at the secondary level:

> **Ester:** Sometimes it's hard to think that far in advance [i.e., secondary school] when they're just in kindergarten, and so I think [having the program extended to the secondary level] made a difference.... With the middle school and in particular now with the high school, we've [gotten a lot of feedback about Spanish grammar]—it's very clear [the students] don't have it. So at the high school, we're doing interventions for that group, but in the meantime we're talking to the middle school, we're talking to the upper [elementary] grade teachers here, about what we need to do differently so we don't end up with kids in the high school that will have a hard time with the A.P. Spanish grammar part, because we didn't teach it to them!
>
> **Interviewer:** And so a lot of that really couldn't be anticipated, not until you...
>
> **Ester:** ... get to that final point [i.e., high school] and you're realizing, "Well, we said we're going to be here [at a certain level of Spanish proficiency], but we're not." And I think then we have an excellent staff that's willing to think and reflect and has the ability to change things.

At the classroom level the importance of collaboration in promoting the cognitive and linguistic development of both majority and minority students has been well established (Brown & Campione, 1994; Dalton, 1998; Faltis & Hudelson, 1998; García, 1993; Gumperz, Cook-Gumperz, & Szymanski, 1999; Lindholm-Leary, 2005; Tharp & Gallimore, 1988; Vygotsky, 1978). In fact, collaboration is a key element in Joint Productive Activity, one of CREDE's five standards for effective pedagogy (Dalton, 1998), in which students and teachers work together to produce a tangible product. Effective collaboration can occur through whole-class lessons, pair work, or cooperative groupings. The project-based learning approach at IAMS lends itself particularly well to this type of collaboration among students, and there are several interesting examples of this type of intellectualism at play in the school. In the primary grades, a typical way of promoting an exchange of ideas is read-alouds, an approach that is used widely in both immersion and mainstream elementary schools. The following example from a second-grade classroom demonstrates how storytelling can be used to promote exchange of ideas as well as higher order thinking and cross-linguistic connections.

Photo by SAGARTdesign

> The teacher reintroduced *La telaraña de Carlota [Charlotte's Web]*, asking for a review of the last chapter that she had read to them. One of the students summarized in Spanish what had happened in the last chapter (which had been read in English—the teacher alternates languages for each chapter). The teacher then started to read. She stopped from time to time to ask students about parts of the chapter, with the students answering in Spanish. "*¿Qué hace Carlota?*" "*¿Las arañas comen insectos?*" "*¿Qué significa escopeta? –pistola?*" "*¿Por qué están engordándole a Wilbur?*" [What is Charlotte making? Do spiders eat insects? What does shotgun mean? —pistol? Why were they fattening up Wilbur?] For this last question, one of the students thought that they were going to kill Wilbur, while others disagreed. The teacher called for a show of hands of the students who thought that they were going to kill Wilbur.

On another day, the same teacher went on to a thematic science unit on spiders, where she used cooperative groupings and integration of language and content to accomplish her objectives in a way that promoted collaboration and exchange across pairs of students.

> After finishing chapter 3 [of *Charlotte's Web*], the teacher returned to the spider booklet project, assigning the students their partners and their books. To form student pairs, the teacher took into account students' interest in particular spiders and their levels of literacy. She paired strong readers and writers with students who struggled with literacy. She also paired boys with boys and girls with girls. She gave each pair of students a book and two pieces of paper, folded to make the booklet, and told them that they would have 2 days to work on the project.
>
> After reading trade books in English on their chosen spider, the students started working on their booklets, where they drew and wrote about the spiders. Students helped each other with their writing, and by the time the class was over, most students had made good progress on preparing their booklets.

In the upper elementary grades at IAMS, persuasive writing tends to be integrated throughout the curriculum, with a heavy emphasis on critical thinking and persuading others to consider different points of view. Some of this is done orally as well as in writing. In-class debates prepare students for persuasive writing. In this way, IAMS teachers promote an exchange of ideas among students that fosters language and literacy development, while also promoting higher order thinking and the ability to understand multiple points of view.

A final example from a fourth-grade classroom at IAMS demonstrates how a teacher can encourage collaboration and an exchange of ideas to promote language and literacy development through a thematic unit that also promotes higher order thinking, integrates language and content objectives, and promotes the use of strategies.

> The teacher instructed the class to put away the books that they were reading and told them that they were going to play a game with words. The point of the game was to practice vocabulary from their thematic unit on the jungle. The teacher asked the class to get out their vocabulary lists from a previous lesson, and then gave index cards

to each group so that the students could write the vocabulary words on them. She demonstrated how she wanted the students to write words on the cards by modeling it on the blackboard. She told them to write in pencil and to not write anything on the back of the card. When they were done, they were supposed to put the cards in the center of the table.

The students began to write the cards, and the teacher interacted with them to see how they were progressing. After 5 minutes, the teacher said that they had to finish in 2 more minutes. They had to write 16 words in all. She then showed them what she wanted them to do next, writing on the back of the index card. She asked, "What sort of words are there?" The students answered adjectives, verbs, and nouns. She asked them to write the part of speech in one corner of the card and told them to ask their classmates if they were uncertain about which type of word it was. A student asked her what type of word *columpiarse* [to swing] was. She answered by telling the student to use it in a sentence: *"Yo me columpio."* [I swing.] By doing this, the student was able to figure out that it was a verb.

She next asked the students to brainstorm with a partner ways in which to organize the words. After the students brainstormed, she wrote their ideas on the board. The ideas they came up with included the following: alphabetical order, whether or not each word had an accent mark, number of letters, number of syllables, part of speech (verb, noun, or adjective), the order of the vocabulary list, or by subtopic within the jungle theme (*orden selvático*). When one student was telling her one of the organizational methods, he broke into English. The teacher told him that he had been doing well in Spanish, encouraging him to return to Spanish. When the student was unable to produce the word *sílaba* [syllable], she whispered it to help him.

She next instructed the class to choose the method that they preferred to organize the words and to then write a funny sentence with the words. She said that they would share their sentences when they were done. She told them that they could choose their own partners, but if they weren't working she would change their partner. She wrote the instructions on the board in Spanish:

1. *Organizar sus palabras.* [Organize your words.]
2. *Formar una oración que incluye muchas palabras.* [Make a sentence that includes a lot of (vocabulary) words.]

A student asked if he could write a story. She answered that she wanted only a sentence. The students spread themselves across the room to work in pairs, some working on the floor and some at tables. The teacher went around to help the pairs. She gave the students large pieces of red and purple paper on which to write their sentences.

A while later, the teacher asked the students to return to their seats. Each pair of students came to the front of the class to read their sentences. Afterward the students put their sentences in the front of the class and placed their cards in their Spanish folders.

Fostering Independence

Fostering independence encourages individuals to extend their learning on their own, without the need for continual prompting and direction from someone else (Kohn, 1999; Resnick & Hall, 2005). Independence is fostered by allowing individuals to make choices about the issues that they pursue, providing them with strategies and skills to work individually, and encouraging self-motivation and self-monitoring, which facilitate the development of initiative and the ability to reflect on one's progress. This applies to both students and teachers. Evelyn Fernández, the assistant principal at Key, summarized these sentiments when she described the impact of the teacher-research project on the participating teachers:

> This was a fantastic project because it demonstrated that teacher-led professional development accomplishes two purposes: improving instruction and improving teachers. The most effective way to improve teachers' behavior is to not only engage them in the process of professional development, but give them control over the experience.... Then teachers can work through a process of trial and error and become better teachers, and that creates a positive ripple effect on students' entire learning experience.
>
> Another great outcome of the project is the development of life-long skills for teachers in terms of keeping their lessons fresh and varied. This is one way to avoid teacher burnout, and it has encouraged our teachers to constantly seek better teaching strategies. The project reinforced their use of assessments to drive instruction and also sharpened their skills in paying attention to how individual children are learning, as in asking themselves, "OK, this child isn't getting it, so let me go back and see how else I can do it." Marleny and Patricia engaged in a lot of reflective teaching, and it made a big difference.

The teachers are more empowered to constantly question and self-assess their teaching skills and strategies. The school's teachers are focused on lessons and skills—but they have to keep in mind that they're teaching kids, so if that kid didn't learn the objectives, it doesn't matter that you taught a perfect lesson. This kind of self-reflection helps them teach the kids and not simply focus on the lesson.

These same themes play out at the classroom level as well. Teachers in effective programs foster independence in their students by providing them with choice and by teaching them skills and strategies that allow them to work independently. Two primary-grade teachers at IAMS discussed the benefits of allowing students to make choices and take ownership of their learning:

A thing that I noticed that really helps is if they can decide as to what they are going to do. You don't have to give them a lot of choices or allow them to change the whole curriculum, but you give them some leeway—choices about the characters they're going to write about, choices about who their partner is going to be. See, that really motivates them, because they're so excited about what they're actually going to create, if it's a fantasy story especially, that they're willing to put in the extra effort and find the words. When they have the idea and they want to go with it, they'll find the means to achieve their goal.

Teachers at all four schools also teach strategies that allow students to work independently. At Key, primary teachers focus on sight words and word families with struggling readers, so that students do not get stuck on those words when reading and get frustrated and give up. When students are writing, the teachers tell them to just write the words the best they can and then make any needed corrections during the editing phase to avoid disrupting their flow of ideas.

One primary teacher at Key spoke about the impact of strategy-based instruction on her students—specifically, that it makes them more independent and gives them more ownership of their own learning.

The kids learn strategies that they can apply on their own. They can self-monitor and they don't always need me right there. You can see sometimes as they think aloud that they are using the strategies. Often it's just asking them, "What do you need to do?" instead of saying, "You need to reread." So they internalize it, and they have more ownership of the process.

Finally, at IAMS, primary teachers discussed strategies to help students, particularly second language learners, derive meaning from text without resorting to translation. In the following quote, a teacher recommended having students test out several possible words in context to see if they made sense:

> In the second grade, you see more of the children developing literacy in their second language. Sometimes they're pretty fluent, particularly the native English speakers in Spanish, although they don't necessarily understand everything that they read. It is important for them to build the meaning of what they're reading. They can't run for the dictionary every single time that they don't understand a word. So it's important to work out approximate meanings of words from context. They also can't always just translate the word immediately into the other language; they also need to build the meaning in the language that they are reading, such as Spanish. This is a challenge, helping the children acquire the understanding and to not do so with translation. One way to do this is to have the children propose possible meanings for the word in the target language and then to try the possibilities in context to see what makes the most sense. It's important to use previous knowledge to get the meaning from context.

Promotion of Higher Order Thinking

The final characteristic of a culture of intellectualism is the promotion of higher order thinking skills. At the program level, teachers, administrators, and parents demonstrate higher order thinking when they meet to problem-solve about a struggling student and to propose alternative instructional techniques, or when teachers learn a technique from mainstream inservice training and modify it for the dual language setting. (See "Fascinating Facts and Remarkable Reports" in chapter 7 for an example of this.)

As discussed previously, primary teachers at Barbieri worked with Lesley University on a literacy initiative. Because the initiative was designed for mainstream programs, the Barbieri teachers had to adapt it to make it useful for their TWI program. This effort was led by one of the bilingual teachers in the TWI program, who had served as the literacy coach for the initiative. She was able to provide demonstrations in Spanish, coach the Spanish-side teachers, and ensure that resources in Spanish matched those in English to the extent possible. Ester de Jong, the assistant director of bilingual education at the time of the study, described the approach and the Barbieri teachers' work with it in the following way, highlighting the synthesis of the literacy initiative with previous knowledge about literacy:

> Basically it's a literacy model ... where you do four types of writing and four types of reading on a daily basis, extensively. You have to have 2 or 3 hours of literacy time and instruction in order to really do it. It's center-based, guided reading, writers workshop, all those kinds of good ... literacy practices. What they've done is really put it in a very systematic framework. It's K–2. We've been fortunate that [one of our teachers] can actually work with both languages, is doing it now in Spanish, and can try to figure out what's different in Spanish as compared to English. And we started thinking about needing blocks of 2 or 3 hours and looking at our model, [and we were concerned with] where are we going to get time?... Knowing what we know about literacy, how should we be [incorporating this program]? I think for us it has confirmed [the wisdom of] doing native language literacy first, as opposed to having a group of students doing it in the second language or to do it even simultaneously. It's the how and when do you introduce a second language part that's been more of the challenge, and as I said, we're rethinking the second grade, using that framework and using it differently.

At the classroom level, the promotion of higher order thinking is a key teaching strategy in immersion classrooms as well as in other types of educational settings for linguistically and culturally diverse students (Echevarria et al., 2004; Howard & Christian, 2002). Not surprisingly, the promotion of higher order thinking is another of CREDE's standards for effective pedagogy (Dalton, 1998) and is an essential component of the Institute for Learning's Principles of Learning (Resnick & Hall, 2005). All students must be prepared to engage in the complex problem solving that will be required of them in their future employment (Levy & Murnane, 2004).

In classrooms, teachers work with students to promote higher order thinking in a number of ways. At the primary level, one of the most common approaches in the domains of oral language and literacy development involves the use of read-alouds, where the teacher reads to the whole class. The following vignette from a first-grade English classroom at Key provides an excellent example of how the teacher can promote higher order thinking in this setting. While providing comprehensible input to make the material accessible to second language learners, the teacher uses multiple modalities to help students understand the content, promoting vocabulary development and relating the content to students' lives (and in this particular case, emphasizing their bilingualism in the process).

> After lunch, the students gather on the floor to read and discuss the story, *The First Thanksgiving*. The teacher asks thought questions on every page, for example, "This is a nonfiction story. Is it true?" and "Who are they talking about in this story?" She also pauses as she reads for kids to guess the next word in the story (e.g., going to *America*).
>
> As they read, the teacher asks the students about ambiguous words, such as spring, and about idiomatic phrases such as, *A guard is posted* (**Teacher:** What does this mean?) and *huddle together* (**Teacher:** Can you show me what it means to huddle together?). She also asks the students to demonstrate the emotion words in the story.
>
> The teacher also makes connections between the students and the characters in the story. She says, "They just said that Squanto speaks English. How is Squanto like you?" The students respond that he is bilingual.

In another example from Key, this time at the upper elementary level, a fourth-grade teacher drew the students' attention to various spelling patterns of words that all had similar sounding endings.

> These were the words in the unit: *sailor, harbor, enter, weather, ladder, cellar, chapter, sugar, supper, collar, motor, favor, bitter, beggar, shower, temper, better, doctor.*
>
> The teacher asked, "What is the tricky part to remember? All of the endings [sound alike], but look at how they're spelled."

At IAMS, upper elementary teachers discussed how they promote higher order thinking and, in particular, how they challenge native speakers while keeping the language level manageable for second language learners. They emphasized the need to be aware of each individual student's capabilities and to tailor instruction and goals in a way that allows each student to work to his or her highest possible level.

> A lot of this management of levels follows from the thematic unit. Teachers have expectations for individual students within the thematic unit and expect them to live up to them. The material that they study lends itself to higher level thinking. The activities are not focused on lectures. If the students don't understand something well enough, we do enough activities in class to get them to understand everything. They do pick it up.
>
> There is a lot of individualized focus and mini-lessons that focus on the needs in specific students. We shoot higher than the kids' ability, and then we support the kids to reach that level. With the Incas, a lot of the vocabulary is very difficult, but we stick with the goal of having them learn that vocabulary. Then we use reading and writing strategies to have them figure out the meaning of the words. We recognize that there are different language levels and that there are different expectations for what is success for different kids.

The following is an example of the type of open-ended activity at IAMS that integrates language and content objectives, promotes higher order thinking, and allows all students to work at their individual levels. In fourth grade, there is an activity called "a paragraph a week," where students write a first-draft paragraph every Monday in response to a question that is related to the unit of study and that is designed to make them think. They then continue to write several drafts over the course of the week to improve their paragraph. In one lesson, the students learned about the solar system and were asked to write about what would happen if there were no sun.

Upper elementary teachers at IAMS also spoke about the impact of standardized testing on the promotion of higher order thinking; in their opinion, the tests discourage critical thinking.

> When you are practicing for standardized tests, using some of the preparation materials, you have to tell the students to stop thinking so critically. Some questions, about 95% of the questions in the world, are open to interpretation. There are often questions in the [instructional] materials that are open to interpretation and for which there

are, accordingly, possible different answers. Our kids are used to using their own interpretation and powers of judgment. We have to tell kids this is the format of the test, you have to figure out what is in the test maker's mind to figure out if it's *a, b, c,* or *d*. Don't think so much as we ask you to do the rest of the year.

It's in a sense another genre, but almost a wasted genre, since they can't use their tremendous powers to analyze, to critique, to evaluate—all of those higher echelon skills that throughout the year we are trying to foster. Now they basically have to forget them.

Finally, the promotion of higher order thinking is also evident at the secondary level. For example, in an eighth-grade classroom at Alicia Chacón, the students did a project on Macbeth in which they read the play, watched the movie, and then performed their own interpretation. Students in that class are used to working in groups and problem-solving real-life situations. There is a clear use of literature and thematic-based studies as a main mode of delivery for the eighth-grade curriculum.

Conclusion

The many examples and quotes shared throughout this chapter demonstrate the ways in which the four highly effective programs profiled here have established cultures of intellectualism and how they use these cultures to promote high levels of bilingualism and biliteracy attainment for their students. In summary, these are the components of a culture of intellectualism that we have discussed:

- **A commitment to ongoing learning**
  - Promoting reflection and change to improve the instructional environment for students
  - Creating an environment in which it is safe for both adults and students to make mistakes and learn from each other
  - Having high expectations for oneself (both adults and students) and others
  - Encouraging students to reflect on their work and to adapt and make changes as needed

- **Collaboration and exchange of ideas**
  - Collaborating and planning with other teachers and sharing challenges and successes
  - Having students collaborate on instructional activities, frequently in pairs or cooperative groups

- **The fostering of independence**
  - Allowing choice and self-initiative in designing curriculum and instructional activities
  - Promoting strategies and skills to allow teachers to investigate areas of interest to them
  - Allowing students to have choice in their topics of study and approaches to accomplishing a task
  - Teaching students strategies to help them work independently

- **The promotion of higher order thinking**
  - Adapting mainstream educational ideas and approaches to a bilingual setting
  - Meeting regularly to discuss issues within the program and how to solve them
  - Fostering critical thinking through a variety of activities, such as project-based instruction and open-ended questions

Chapter 5:
Promoting Bilingualism and Biliteracy Through a Culture of Equity

Introduction

Promoting equity among students from diverse backgrounds is one of the foundational principles of TWI education (Howard & Christian, 2002; Lindholm-Leary, 2001, 2005). TWI programs go beyond the mere desegregation of minority students to the active integration of diverse students and promotion of the languages and cultures of all of the participants (Freeman, 1998; Glenn, 1990). Integration is based on a belief that isolating English language learners in separate programs or schools is not beneficial to their academic, social, or emotional growth, and that the perspectives and skills of minority students are assets to all students in the integrated classroom (Brisk, 2006). Developing bilingualism and biliteracy in equal measures in native English speakers and speakers of the partner language is valued because all students deserve to reap the benefits of bilingualism for cognitive and social development and to increase their skills for the future workplace.

Because of the integration of students from different cultural and linguistic backgrounds, an explicit goal of TWI programs is to develop positive cross-cultural attitudes in students (Howard & Christian, 2002). Specifically, TWI programs strive to give all students the opportunity to

- Strengthen their sense of their own cultural and language identity
- Strengthen their ability to form and sustain friendships across cultures and languages

- Develop resilience in the face of prejudice and exclusion aimed at them and their own language or ethnic group
- Develop cross-cultural mediation and conflict-resolution skills
- Develop awareness of privilege and power dynamics among various language and cultural groups (Olsen, 2005)

To establish and nurture a culture of equity, TWI programs must overcome pressures from the wider American society, which, in general, does not value the languages or cultures of students from diverse backgrounds and emphasizes English language proficiency above all else as the route to academic success in the United States (Brisk, 2006). Teachers also face the challenge of curriculum mandates that seem to leave little room for multicultural themes (Anberg-Espinosa, 2006). As noted in other chapters of this book, the four schools profiled here have not achieved perfect equity in all aspects of their program. However, the ability of the teachers in the focus groups to articulate their feelings about those issues and suggest ways that they are trying to work around the program's weaknesses are a strong testament to their reflectiveness, to their intention of empowerment, and to their awareness of the importance of promoting equity in the school and beyond (Lindholm-Leary, 2005).

At the four schools profiled in this book, a culture of equity is demonstrated at the program and classroom levels through (a) the active promotion of the partner language and culture, (b) the inclusion of students with special learning needs, (c) balanced attention to the needs of native speakers and those of second language learners, and (d) a focus on multiculturalism. Balancing the realities of societal and pedagogical pressures with their own philosophies of education for minority students, TWI practitioners explicitly create an educational environment where all students' backgrounds and abilities are valued and cultivated, and where the study of cultures and languages beyond those represented in the school is also actively encouraged.

Valuing and Promoting the Partner Language and Culture

Because the English language and European-American culture are such powerful influences in the United States, even in tight-knit immigrant communities, demonstrating equity in TWI programs means implicitly valuing and actively promoting the partner language and culture(s) at both the school and classroom levels. This is based on one of the fundamental motivations behind TWI, which is to promote large-scale social change by elevating the status of the partner language and culture within the walls of individual schools (Freeman, 1998).

Linguistic Equity in the TWI School

At the school level, program administrators need to consider linguistic equity at all stages of program planning and implementation and at both the macro and micro levels. Decisions about the school population, staffing, use of the partner language in school-wide activities, and assessment all have an impact on equity.

TWI programs try to balance their population by native language, aiming to achieve a 50/50 ratio of native English to native Spanish speakers in each classroom. Thus, in theory, the Spanish dominance of half of the children will create an atmosphere in which at least half of the students will want to speak Spanish most of the time and therefore encourage the English speakers to do so as well. However, the language dominance as determined by entrance assessments or home language surveys does not necessarily reflect the reality of how students talk with one another in school. One teacher noted that students who were identified as native Spanish speakers by language tests in first grade were speaking primarily in English to each other that same year. According to a first-grade Spanish teacher,

> When they [native Spanish speakers] are talking with each other, it's over 90% in English. And especially socially, on the playground, it's probably 99% English. When they're talking in the classroom to each other, then a little bit more Spanish creeps in, but still English dominates between the students.

The concerns of the participants about language use are echoed in numerous studies of TWI programs (Carrigo, 2000; Delgado-Larocco, 1998; Griego-Jones, 1994; Hadi-Tabassum, 2006; Howard & Christian, 1997; Potowski, 2002), which indicate that in spite of educators' best efforts to enhance the status and use of Spanish, English remains the dominant language used by students.

Three of the four schools in our studies use selection procedures and lotteries that ensure that they will start with a cohort of students that is balanced by native language group. (IAMS has a lottery based on race/ethnicity because of a desegregation mandate.) The kindergarten cohort can be weighted, if necessary, to ensure that attrition over the course of the program does not unbalance the classes beyond the two-thirds/one-third ratio recommended for TWI programs (Howard & Christian, 2002). Each of the four focal schools is a program of choice (open to all students in the district or a region within the district), which is an advantage when the surrounding neighborhood does not provide a balance of native speakers of the two languages.

Additionally, the four schools allow native Spanish speakers to enter the program at any grade level. The rationale for this policy is that, in addition to the benefit for incoming native Spanish speakers of continuing their education in their native language, the presence of such students can be conducive to use of the partner language at school; both native English speakers and native Spanish speakers are forced, at least at first, to speak Spanish with the newcomers. In fact, at IAMS, this factor was particularly promoted as the school developed an exchange program with students from Michoacán, Mexico, so that their upper elementary students could have the opportunity to engage in authentic conversations in the visitors' dominant language. In contrast, the four schools do not allow non-Spanish-speaking students to enter the program after first grade, because they would likely not be able to make fast enough gains in Spanish to do grade-level work.

Selecting teachers with appropriate training and experience and who demonstrate a commitment to TWI has been cited by many TWI practitioners as a critical factor in the effectiveness of a program (Sugarman & Howard, 2001). Further, a small number of studies of teachers' experiences in TWI programs (reviewed in Howard, Sugarman, et al., 2003) indicate that personal motivation based on past negative experiences as linguistic minorities and a commitment to elevating the status of minority languages and cultures are strong themes in teachers' reflections on their involvement in TWI education. The following quote demonstrates this in terms of how a Spanish teacher at Barbieri viewed the connection between teacher commitment and success of the program, particularly for linguistic minority students:

> I think Barbieri has some really good teachers. You see someone like [my colleague], she's so passionate about teaching and [the] Spanish [language]. Next year I'm going to be working with [someone] who's a fourth-grade English teacher, and again, she's a native English speaker but she's just so passionate about the culture.... Last night she went to the Museum of Fine Arts to watch a film on Mexican immi-

grants in New York ... and just to do that, to be interested in a different culture and really want to help them, is amazing.

A couple of times we've hired people that aren't that way, and that just doesn't work. I interviewed someone a couple weeks ago and I said, "You know, I'm going to be honest with you: Teaching is hard, teaching second language learners is very hard, and teaching in a two-way bilingual program can be crazy." It's a hard job. And the only thing that keeps you going—you don't have to be ... the best teacher in the world—I'm still not great teaching and it's my fourth year—but you have to be passionate ... and you have to be here wanting to help Hispanic kids because those are the kids that really, really need you. And I said to her, "If you don't have that passion ... if you're not dying to work with this population, this is just not the job for you. I don't care so much about the methods of teaching—you'll learn that, you'll try things that work and don't work, and if it doesn't work you'll change it, who cares?—but you need to be passionate about doing it and wanting to help the Spanish speakers."

Another way that programs promote a bilingual atmosphere is by including both Spanish and English in school-wide routines. For example, at Alicia Chacón, the Pledge of Allegiance is recited in English and Spanish successively; Key uses Spanish and English on alternating days for the Pledge and other announcements. Because the TWI program at Barbieri is a strand within a school, announcements there are made in English, but several interviewees noted that it would go a long way toward promoting diversity at the school if more school-wide announcements and activities were in Spanish.

Schools also strive to promote the Spanish language by having abundant, high-quality materials available in Spanish. This is a difficult issue for many schools, because materials brought from abroad are often culturally or linguistically inappropriate for bilingual learners in the United States, but better materials are simply unavailable. A teacher at Alicia Chacón noted that "there has been an improvement and much more is available than before, but quality Spanish [materials are] hard to come by."

Finally, conducting summative assessments in both languages of the program promotes equity. When Spanish-language tests are seen as less important than tests administered in English, it sends the message that the Spanish language itself is less important (McCollum, 1999). Furthermore, to see that the goals of bilingualism and biliteracy are being accomplished at the program level, schools need to measure and report students' growth in both languages (Howard, Lindholm-Leary, et al., 2005; Howard, Sugarman, Perdomo, & Adger, 2005). Of our four focal schools, only Alicia Chacón is located in a state where state-mandated tests are offered in Spanish, and both native English speakers and native Spanish speakers at that school avail themselves of the option to take the tests in Spanish. Although state-mandated tests in Virginia are available only in English, administrators working with Key and the other TWI schools in the district made Spanish language and literacy assessment an important part of their district-mandated program evaluation. They conducted language and literacy assessments in both languages and reported on both to the school board. Finally, during the time of our study, Barbieri gave the *Aprenda* standardized test in Spanish to its third and fifth graders as a matter of course.

Test preparation is a big issue when it comes to outside pressures that reduce the quality of instruction in both languages, but particularly Spanish. An IAMS teacher mentioned,

> Time that used to be devoted to more critical thinking skills in Spanish was becoming, in many cases, devoted to test preparation questions, which are only in English. Test preparation definitely takes away from class time. It also forces the teachers to use more English, since test preparation is in English.

Before the 2004 Massachusetts initiative that effectively eliminated some forms of bilingual education in the state, Barbieri staff were petitioning the state to accept their Spanish reading and math scores. As Ester de Jong noted, "As long as they still consider ... the presence of the native language like a crutch and somehow it's going to contaminate the scores, we have a battle on our hands for that one." For all four schools—even Alicia Chacón, which is the only school involved in the study that had its Spanish test scores "count"—making sure students are able to score well in English is a pressure that has only increased over the last few years.

Promoting the Use of Spanish in the Classroom

The program design and the choices made by administrators to foster the use of Spanish at the school level are important factors in the culture of equity, but it is what happens at the classroom level that ensures that the quantity and quality of Spanish instruction are sufficient to develop bilingualism and biliteracy in all children. In the literature on immersion education, the separation of languages in the classroom is often cited as a necessary condition for the promotion of bilingualism and biliteracy, although it is recognized that students in the primary grades are likely to be unable to produce extended discourse exclusively in their second language (Cloud et al., 2000; Howard & Christian, 2002). There has also been increasing awareness of the fact that this is not a clear-cut issue, and that there are situations in which it is useful to use both program languages together for academic or social reasons (Cummins, 2006; Hadi-Tabassum, 2006; Howard, Sugarman, et al., 2005). In the focus groups, teachers were unanimous in their general agreement with the principle of separation of languages; however, they noted that because of the dominance of English in society, a more salient feature of promoting bilingualism and biliteracy than separation of languages was maximizing the use of Spanish. Teachers in three of the four schools (the exception being Alicia Chacón, located in southwest Texas on the Mexican border) believed that because students heard so much English outside of school, it was crucial for teachers not to speak English during Spanish time and for them to encourage the students to use Spanish as much as possible. As one teacher said, they go to great lengths to avoid code-switching (into English) because "it's like water in a dike once water starts slipping through. English is just everywhere in society. If you start code-switching, the flood of English will just come." The teachers in the focus groups were unified in their belief that time allotted to Spanish should not be lost by speaking English; the use of Spanish during English instructional time was not as great a concern.

Nevertheless, there are important pedagogical and sociolinguistic reasons for teachers to speak strictly in one language or the other most of the time. Several teachers noted how important this was, because "if information is presented first in English and later in Spanish, then many students will tune out the Spanish." None of the teachers in the focus groups repeat lessons in both languages; however, the use of thematic instruction, which is particularly emphasized at IAMS, allows students to hear vocabulary and concepts in both languages within a short time span.

Teachers at all four schools reported that they rely on students to use each other for assistance when they need a translation, and they try very hard to use only the language designated for that time. There are some exceptions to this rule, however. The same teacher quoted earlier who referred to the "flood" of English said,

> I have had cases where a child is brand new [to the school], and has no Spanish, and it causes some strain on the system. So ... what I've done, when he became upset and he really needed some individual attention from the teacher, I left the classroom and had a brief discussion with him, trying to help him, calm him down, get him reoriented in English, because it wouldn't have worked in Spanish, and then we went back in. So we really do try as a school to go to great lengths to stay in the target language.

Most instruction is delivered monolingually, with occasional and very specific uses of the other language to clarify the meanings of concepts or to give students the vocabulary they will need if they are going to be tested in English because of local or state mandates. Another exception concerns cognates: Teachers are able to broaden their students' vocabulary and enhance their metalinguistic awareness by pointing out cognates and false cognates that they encounter in their reading. This approach is supported by research that has found explicit cognate instruction to be effective for bilingual learners, particularly native Spanish speakers (Carlo et al., 2004). Teachers also try to accommodate parents who have difficulty helping their children with homework in a language the parents don't understand. An IAMS teacher noted that, on parental request, and particularly for math, "I've given parents the worksheets in English, but I've said specifically, 'These aren't for the kids. These are for you to help, but the child has to do it on the Spanish sheet.'"

Teaching to a mixed class of native speakers and second language learners can be a daunting task. But teachers in several of the focus groups reported feeling confident of their ability to make themselves understood by all their students through the use of appropriate sheltered instruction techniques (see Echevarria et al., 2004, and chapter 2 of this volume). They also know that students rely on each other for translations and other help. Although they didn't want students to become overly reliant on their peers for translation, having a mixed-language group freed the teachers from being their students' only bilingual model and allowed them to adhere to the designated language of instruction. Teachers also acknowledged that monolingual delivery of instruction was effective even for the students who appeared the least proficient in their second language because, in many cases, they understood more of the language than they were able to produce.

Promoting Bilingualism for Students With Special Needs

A culture of equity is also demonstrated in student selection procedures at the four schools, all of which include students with special learning needs. Program administrators and teachers spoke of the imperative to meet the needs of all students, using whatever resources the school has available. This reflects current research on the benefits of including linguistically diverse students with special needs in bilingual programs (Genesee, Paradis, & Crago, 2004; Ortiz & Yates, 2002).

At Alicia Chacón, students with special needs are welcomed into the program, and adjustments such as special education pullout classes and in-classroom support are made to accommodate them. In addition, all students have access to a Tutoring and Learning Center designed especially for occasions when children need additional support in classroom or homework activities. If a student is not successful at learning in the specialized and demanding environment of the TWI program, the school offers ample opportunities for success (as in sessions with parents and other interventions) before a student is considered for transfer from the program, which administrators say is a rare occurrence.

Key School staff have also taken steps to ensure equity for students of all ability levels. Before it became a whole-school program (1995–1996) under the leadership of current principal Marjorie Myers, there were no special education students in the program. Ms. Myers decided to make the program inclusive for all students and began allowing students with special education needs to enroll in the 1996–1997 academic year. Hiring both English and Spanish special education teachers made it possible for special education students from both native language backgrounds to participate. As one teacher said with regard to native Spanish speakers with special needs, "It's not fair to penalize native Spanish speakers by not letting them learn Spanish—their heritage, their lives." Key students are accepted without regard to special needs, and special education services are available on a pullout basis to students on the basis of test scores and teacher recommendations.

Like Key, IAMS enrolls students on the basis of a lottery and does not exclude students with special education needs. These needs are generally identified after the student has been enrolled for some time and seems to be experiencing difficulty in the classroom despite receiving targeted ESL, SSL, or reading interventions, as appropriate. Students who are identified as having special needs generally receive special education services via a special education teacher who assists them in their regular TWI classroom.

In addition to the special education services that are offered in conjunction with the mainstream program at the school, Barbieri has a special program, Sage, for children in Grades 2–5 who are very creative and think abstractly. For a time, few Spanish speakers were being accepted to the program because placement testing was conducted in English, and the nature of referral criteria (with more vocal parents pushing to have their children assessed for the program) favored native English speakers. However, several years ago, school personnel began working to make the process less linguistically and culturally biased, again demonstrating awareness of and reflection on equity issues in their program.

As is frequently noted in the literature on English language learners with learning disabilities, it is very important that a diagnosis of disability be made on the basis of students' performance in their native language (Genesee et al., 2004). Bilingual programs, including the four we are profiling, have an advantage over other types of education in that teachers have regular opportunities to observe students learning in their native language and to collect assessment data in both languages. According to one teacher at Barbieri, with the opportunity to teach native Spanish speakers in their native language, "It is easier to sort out at an early age when a child is having difficulties, learning disabilities. Sometimes it can take years before you find out if it is a problem with the language or a learning disability, so I find it to be a huge advantage."

Balancing the Needs of Native English Speakers and Native Spanish Speakers

As indicated above, balancing English and Spanish instruction is a major challenge in TWI programs, but this goes beyond the time allocation of English and Spanish for instruction; it goes to the heart of whether the needs of both native English speakers and native Spanish speakers are being met. At the program level, this challenge is reflected in the choice of program model, the language allocation policy, the materials used in the curriculum, and testing. In the classroom, the needs of both groups of students are taken into consideration by enriching the language development of native speakers while sheltering instruction for second language learners.

Reflecting on Balance in the Program

Concern over meeting the needs of both language groups was felt strongly by the faculty at Barbieri. At the inception of the program, they decided to implement a model in which initial literacy instruction would be conducted in homogenous native language groups. There was philosophical agreement among program staff that doing so would be beneficial for both native English speakers and native Spanish speakers in their community. These practitioners felt that providing initial literacy instruction in Spanish to native English speakers might be less effective for Barbieri's diverse population than research had shown it to be for middle-class White students (de Jong, 2002). They also felt that keeping the two native language groups separate for initial literacy instruction would enable the Spanish teachers to deliver instruction to the native Spanish speakers at a higher level and a faster pace, without the need to cater to the very basic Spanish needs of the entering native English speakers. In other words, they perceived this approach to be the most effective one for promoting high levels of achievement in both of their student populations. (As noted in the postscript in chapter 8, they are currently reconsidering this decision.)

One important feature of Barbieri's program administration is that consideration for language allocation and curriculum are continually revisited, and changes are made based on the needs of each cohort. The former administrator of Barbieri's TWI program, Ester de Jong, explained that at one time, some of the rigidity of the program model was rethought because native Spanish speakers seemed ready to begin formal English language arts earlier than it was being offered. She reasoned that "some of the kids are ready to do literacy in English after first grade, and so they should be doing that. I think we've been holding it back longer just because of the model." It was decided that students should be transitioned from an ESL/oral language development curriculum to one emphasizing formal literacy skills as soon as they were ready, even as early as second grade.

Other evidence of reflection on whether the program model meets all students' needs was offered by the Spanish teachers at Key, who expressed dissatisfaction about the inequity of time and resources that were allotted to language arts in the two languages. One Spanish teacher remarked, with regard to the priorities for the Spanish half of the day, "Math comes first, science comes second, and language arts comes third, when you have time." In contrast, because of testing and other mandates, language arts is a priority in English and has always had ample time devoted to it. As a result of ongoing conversations and evidence from the district's program evaluation, school leaders decided that at least half an hour of Spanish time had to be directed to formal language arts. The Commonwealth of Virginia recommends 120 minutes a day of language arts instruction in Grades K–2 and 90 minutes a day in Grades 3–5. The principal decided to divide the required amount of language arts instruction between English and Spanish, allotting 60–90 minutes for English and 30 minutes for Spanish.

Teachers at Key also noted the inequality of teaching Spanish language arts in a whole-group setting rather than using the flexible pullout grouping in place for English language arts. One primary-grade teacher noted that it's difficult "to meet every kid at his level" with 20 to 25 students in the class, even if the students are working in groups. To attempt to remedy this situation, the principal has placed ESOL/HILT (English for Speakers of Other Languages/High Intensity Language Training) assistants and special education teachers in the Spanish classes. In addition, a Spanish assistant from the Embassy of Spain works in the classrooms with Spanish teachers to support the students, especially the native English speakers. But staffing problems cannot easily be corrected because, as is the case for all schools in the district, staffing allocations are based solely on student enrollment figures; Key is not given any additional staffing resources for the immersion program.

Finally, the upper-grade Spanish teachers don't have the benefit of Spanish language test scores to help them make appropriate decisions concerning Spanish language arts placement and instruction. They have few resources compared to those that are available to support English language arts. The teachers at Key were of one voice about the importance of this issue for their school and the need to find ways to address it. As a result of a recent program evaluation, the school and district administration have also prioritized this issue, recommending the development of a Spanish language arts framework; the development of assessments to determine language dominance; and the implementation of consistent, informal oral language assessments and formal mid-year and end-of-year Spanish writing assessments (Forbes-Ullrich & Perdomo, 2005).

Teaching a Diverse Population Through Integrated and Homogenous Grouping

When teaching in heterogeneous groups, teachers use various techniques to ensure that they are understood, to encourage students to take risks in their language, and to meet the language- and content-learning needs of both native speakers and second language learners. The use of sheltered instruction strategies (Echevarria et al., 2004) allows teachers to make content comprehensible for language learners while keeping the academic content challenging. Teachers from each of the four schools mentioned many such strategies that they use (see chapter 2).

When native speakers and second language learners are integrated, there are sociocultural benefits to their interaction. TWI teachers have a unique opportunity to encourage native Spanish speakers to see themselves as and to act as language experts for their peers. As one first-grade teacher at IAMS explained,

> I think one thing that's important for the kids who are learning English as their second language is . . . that they get an extra boost of self-confidence because they're the experts [in Spanish]. Years ago I had a girl in my first-grade class who was very dominant in Spanish, and she was one of the only kids who was very reticent about even trying to say a word in English. But the wonderful thing in her case was that she had a lot of pride about her Spanish skills. And she got to be one of the experts in the class, because everyone knew that she spoke Spanish very well and that she had a good vocabulary. So whenever they needed help with their Spanish, they turned to her.... If you've ever been in any kind of a transitional bilingual program, it's a whole different story. [Spanish speakers are] the minority and in [our program] they're the majority in the terms of having the power [because] the target language here [is] Spanish and not English, so they have an expertise. In terms of getting her or someone like her to feel comfortable with their English, we promote self-confidence, like "Wow, look what you can do."

Beyond the affective needs of minority students, teachers can meet language development needs of both groups of students by encouraging them to take risks with the language so that they can push themselves to produce at the highest level possible. A teacher at Alicia Chacón explained that she does this by

> providing recognition to the child when they are showing an attempt to use the language. Some students shy away from the language, so making a big celebration out of it is not necessary, but recognizing that they are doing well and constantly modeling the target language are

keys to getting the students to use the language. The open and flexible atmosphere removes a lot of situations where students refuse to
use the target language.

Teachers also provide frequent opportunities for students to present their
work to their peers so that all of them get used to seeing others taking risks
in their second language and not being criticized for making mistakes.

An increasing number of TWI programs are separating students by native
language for initial literacy instruction (Center for Applied Linguistics, 2006).
Although this approach has not been well documented or researched, the
concern voiced by IAMS and Barbieri teachers, who use this approach, relates
to the different needs of native speakers and second language learners in the
development of literacy. As noted earlier, at Barbieri in particular, there was a
concern that Spanish instruction would be watered down for the benefit of
the native English speakers. It was very important to program staff that native
Spanish speakers be given the same academic and linguistic challenges in
their native language that native English speakers are given in theirs. As one
Spanish teacher said, "I want to give them [big] vocabulary … words that
they can use in their writing, and that makes no sense for the English speakers [because] they're not there yet." When working in heterogeneous groups,
this Spanish teacher felt it was important to continue not to water down her
instruction, but instead to use sheltered instruction strategies such as rephras-
ing, drawing on the board, and using gestures and manipulatives.

At IAMS, students also receive initial literacy instruction in groups determined by language dominance. The following vignette demonstrates the
kind of extended, sophisticated discourse that would be difficult to sustain
in a heterogeneous group.

> In her first-grade Spanish-for-native-speakers group, the teacher was
> having the students review the story, *"Timmy en el circo"* ["Timmy at
> the Circus"] that they had read the previous day in their basal reader,
> *Cataplum.* She had them tell her everything that they could remember
> that had happened in the story and wrote what they said on a large
> newsprint pad on an easel. The students took turns telling her what to
> write. She asked them questions to get them to furnish her more infor-
> mation, for example, *"¿Qué más pasaba al principio del cuento?* [What
> else happened at the beginning of the story?]." When a student inter-
> rupted a fellow student, she said, *"Déjalo decir, vamos a poner en
> orden después* [Let him talk, we'll put it in order later]."

The students gave her the following sentences, which she wrote on the newsprint:

> *El dueño del circo estaba triste.*
> *El león estaba triste porque extrañaba a su selva.*
> *La cebra estaba triste porque se sentía sola.*
> *El payaso estaba triste porque nada le hacía reír.*
> *Entonces Timmy les ayudó.*
> *Primero pintó una selva en la jaula donde estaba*
>   *el león y le puso una radio para que*
>   *escuchara sonidos de la selva.*
> *Luego Timmy le pintó rayas al caballo para que*
>   *la cebra no se sintiera tan sola.*

[The owner of the circus was sad.
The lion was sad because he missed his jungle.
The zebra was sad because he felt lonely.
The clown was sad because nothing made him laugh.
Then Timmy helped them.
First he painted a jungle in the lion's cage and gave
   him a radio so he could listen to the sounds of the
   jungle.
Then Timmy painted stripes on the horse so the zebra
   would not feel so alone.]

At this point, the teacher helped a student to say what happened next, by saying, *"Dígalo del parte de Timmy y no de payaso* [Tell about what Timmy did, not the clown]." The student ended up giving her the following sentence, which she added to the many already on the board: *"Luego Timmy se resbaló en la cáscara de plátano y el payaso se rió* [Then Timmy slipped on the banana peel and the clown laughed]." When the next student proposed, *"El dueño le dejó hacer que Timmy se llamó maestro de ceremonias* [The owner let Timmy become the master of ceremonies]," the teacher helped the student to rephrase and expand the response. She wrote *"El dueño era muy contento y le hizo maestro de ceremonias a Timmy* [The owner was very happy and made Timmy master of ceremonies]."

After they finished writing the story, she assigned the students partners and told them to choose one of the sentences to write and illustrate together. She gave them a large piece of paper to do their artwork. As the students worked on their illustration projects, the teacher went around to see how they were doing and to offer help as needed.

Clearly, there are affective and cognitive benefits in both integrated and homogenous groupings. Integrated groups allow students to use each other as resources, to be role models and see their peers as models, and to take risks with the language when they see their peers doing so, thus giving them important opportunities to practice their second language (Cloud et al., 2000; Curtain & Dahlberg, 2003). Homogeneous groupings enable teachers to target instruction to the specific needs of each native language group. Effective programs, such as the four profiled here, use a combination of both approaches at different times and for different purposes.

Fostering an Appreciation for Multiculturalism

Diversity Within the School

Promotion of an appreciation for the diversity found within their schools is a defining characteristic of TWI programs. Explicit attention is drawn to linguistic diversity by the use of two languages for instruction. To broaden the idea of linguistic diversity to include an awareness of cultural diversity, IAMS takes an approach that makes the connection between language and culture explicit. As one teacher explained,

> Learning about another culture has so much to do with learning a language. Resisting the other language, the student is insulting the culture of half of the class. If a student doesn't like the other language, it's really not OK to express it and it's important to try to get them to see the good and the positive in that language.

Because students value each other as individuals, seeing a link between language and culture can help them see the value in learning their second language as a way to understand the perspectives of their peers.

In addition to appreciating cross-linguistic differences, students come to appreciate the differences within their own linguistic groups as well. At Key, one of the upper-grade teachers noted that

A Mexican little girl talked to me in the *tú* [the familiar form of *you*], and this other Salvadoran girl said, "No! You talk to her as *usted* [the formal form of *you*]. You don't say *tú* to the teacher." So they had this argument. [Laughter] So even the native Spanish speakers can learn from each other.

There is, understandably, some tension in trying to integrate the two groups of students while promoting pride in their own heritage and distinctiveness. A teacher at Barbieri noted that she had mixed feelings about students choosing to associate with those who are like them:

For example, the Spanish speakers and the English speakers segregate themselves during lunch, and they sit with all Hispanic kids here, all the English-speaking kids here, and then all girls and all boys. At first I was like, why is that happening? Can we figure out a way [to change it]?... And then I said to myself, but wait, I have Puerto Rican friends, and often I want to get together with them and do our Puerto Rican things! If they're together mixed up all day long … maybe they just want to be alone for a [while]… and then I thought, well maybe that's fine, but then I go back and forth and think, but they should be playing together.… It's hard, I can't figure it out.

Nevertheless, Barbieri is successful in developing bilingualism to the point that the distinctions between the language groups can be hard to make. The second-grade Spanish teacher at Barbieri said that one of the greatest successes of the program is

just seeing the level—as the kids have gotten into the upper grades—of verbal fluency, oral fluency, and they're speaking with an accent that you can't distinguish if they're Hispanic or they're Anglo. That is very inspiring. I actually video[-taped] one of my kids' presentations, and that's one of the most moving things, in that people … see the kid and then ask, "Well, is he an Anglo or is he Hispanic?" It was cool.

Culture in the Curriculum

Studying foreign cultures is mandatory in most curricula throughout the United States, but TWI programs incorporate students' and teachers' own experiences as well. A primary-grade teacher at IAMS noted that "We try to make them [the students] feel very proud of who they are and where they come from. [We say,] 'Oh, you come from Puerto Rico, tell us about it'— motivating them to feel good about it." Her colleague added, "We put that in the curriculum, too. In each grade, we do curriculum that draws on their family background." Teachers often discuss their own diverse backgrounds with the students as well. In one lesson using the text *Tradiciones [Traditions]*, a Spanish teacher at Key took the opportunity to discuss the different names for *guacamole* in different countries and interjected comments about his home country and how they treat guests in their home.

Alicia Chacón promotes not just biculturalism, but multiculturalism, in that students study Chinese, German, Japanese, or Russian in a 30- to 45-minute class every day. These courses are taught by a native of the country

Photo by Nancy Ryan

where the language is spoken, and the regular classroom teachers try to infuse cultural learning about the country into the curriculum. The knowledge that students acquire about those countries can be applied to other projects as well, as described in the vignette in chapter 6 in which eighth-grade students were asked to design a new government for Afghanistan and were directed to consider their past learning about the forms of government in China, Germany, Japan, and Russia.

Cultural learning is a rich area for integrating language and content. One fourth-grade teacher at Alicia Chacón integrated a social studies lesson for Black History Month with a book, *The Drinking Gourd,* that was used for language arts study at the same time. On Day 2 of this thematic unit, after reviewing the story they had read as a group the day before, students wrote two or three paragraphs giving their personal opinions about the story. They were asked, "Did the characters do the right thing helping slaves to escape? But they broke the law, therefore what do you think? What would you have done?" The teacher also had a project where students researched the countries of origin of various characters in the story they were reading, looking for information on the country's climate and landform and other information that would be significant for a visitor to that country.

Learning about different cultures is also an area that lends itself to experiential learning, demonstrations, and parental involvement. A class of third graders at IAMS who were about to study the Incas were asked to draw ideas from observing the fifth grade's exhibition on the Aztecs. At the exhibition in the school gym, they saw a performance of Aztec dancing and visited exhibits with Aztec arts, crafts, and foods.

The December holidays offer a particularly good opportunity to involve parents, as one second-grade teacher at Barbieri said:

> I have them during the holidays talk about the different holidays. I'll typically have a mom come in and we'll do Chanukah, potato latkes. I had a mom come in and do Kwanzaa, a mom come in and talk about Christmas ... whatever cultural contributions they can make, and if it involves teaching in the classroom or cooking or whatever, we get them involved that way.

Likewise, students in a second-grade class at IAMS used their prior knowledge of American culture to write in Spanish about the various holidays that fall in December. They were observed writing about Kwanzaa in Spanish for a contribution to a book they were creating about the December celebrations of various cultures. It is important to note that these types of holiday-oriented celebrations are just one part of the programs' overall attention to promoting multiculturalism, as on their own, holiday celebrations can be somewhat superficial and serve to reinforce rather than challenge cultural stereotypes (Brisk, 2006).

Conclusion

Teachers involved in the study were very aware of the dominance of English among the students and the need for a conscious effort on the part of school personnel to encourage greater use of Spanish. The teachers saw themselves as part of a struggle to get students to speak Spanish, but from their comments it was clear that they viewed this struggle as more sociopolitical than pedagogical: They saw that their students could understand and in most cases produce comprehensible Spanish, but that outside pressures—from peers, parents, testing and curriculum mandates, U.S. society—make it difficult for students to resist the pull toward English. Indeed, the perspective of the teachers in the focus groups ran counter to the perspective of many Americans, who believe that Spanish speakers are reluctant to learn or speak English. What teachers saw as a problem was not the students' lack of desire to speak English but their lack of motivation to speak Spanish.

To summarize, the teachers' and programs' nurturing of a culture of equity in order to promote bilingualism and biliteracy for all students was seen in the following ways:

- **Valuing and protecting time for the partner language and its associated culture(s)**
  - Attempting to have equal numbers of students from each language background
  - Elevating the minority language and native speakers of that language
  - Including both languages in school-wide routines
  - Conducting assessments in both languages
  - Separating languages with occasional "over promotion" of Spanish
  - Relying on students to provide peer translation and second language support

- **Promoting bilingualism for students with special needs**
  - Allowing all students to enroll in the program
  - Providing needed supports for students with special learning needs
  - Monitoring language and literacy development in the native language relative to that in the second language

- **Balancing the needs of native English speakers and native Spanish speakers**
  - Attending to balance and appropriate implementation of language arts instruction in two languages
  - Differentiating instruction, which sometimes results in homogeneous groupings by native language or language dominance

- **Fostering an appreciation for multiculturalism**
  - Promoting awareness of and pride in the multiple cultures represented within the program
  - Calling attention to cultural variation as well as linguistic variation
  - Using study of language and study of culture in mutually reinforcing ways
  - Promoting integration of language and content instruction through cultural themes

Chapter 6: Promoting Bilingualism and Biliteracy Through a Culture of Leadership

Introduction

The importance of strong leadership in promoting strong academic outcomes for students has well been established in both the mainstream literature and literature on the education of linguistic and cultural minorities. Research has shown that when there is strong district-level support, strong onsite leadership from the principal or program coordinator or lead teacher, and shared leadership among school administrators, teachers, and parents, students tend to perform better (Lindholm-Leary, 2005).

Less attention, however, has been paid to how leadership plays out at the classroom level, with teachers promoting leadership abilities in their students and developing an atmosphere of consensus building and shared leadership in the classroom. Similarly, the impact of a strong culture of leadership on the specific outcomes of language and literacy development has been left largely unexplored. Data collected for the various studies described in this book reveal four ways that a culture of leadership can be manifested in successful TWI programs, both at the program level and the classroom level:

- Taking initiative (seeking out information and resources, advocating for the program, promoting change)
- Making public presentations (sharing ideas by speaking or writing in public venues)

- Responding to the needs of others
- Building consensus and sharing leadership

These four themes will be explored in the following sections, with ample vignettes from TWI classrooms and excerpts from interviews and focus groups with teachers, parents, and administrators to support and contextualize our assertions.

Taking Initiative

At the program level, effective teachers, administrators, and parents are empowered to shape program design and implementation, select appropriate resources, and identify priorities for the recruitment and professional development of teachers. All of these forms of agency promote the stronger development of bilingualism and biliteracy among the students.

First, in the area of program design and implementation, strong programs tend to have key leaders who were instrumental in founding the programs and in helping them to grow and develop. Minerva Gonzalez, a second-grade teacher at Barbieri, explains her involvement in the development of the TWI program:

> We were really just tired of "us" and "them" and we wanted to have an "ours" approach as far as the children are concerned. They are everyone's responsibility, not just the bilingual teachers'. The two-way was a way of merging standard and bilingual staff, students, and parent population. These sentiments led us to write a grant and, lo and behold, we got it. That was the beginning of the two-way. It has evolved and grown and it's now in its 10th year, so I've been involved from the very beginning.

As is the case with many who are motivated to start TWI programs, Minerva and others at Barbieri were concerned about the limitations and negative consequences of having an isolated, transitional bilingual program for the native Spanish speakers. They took the initiative to change the situation for the better by writing a grant to initiate a TWI program.

Leaders of established TWI programs continue to reflect on the program and promote needed changes to keep the program strong. This is what happened at Barbieri with the hiring of Susan McGilvray as director of bilingual education for the district of Framingham. Ester de Jong, her assistant director at the time of the study, commented on Susan's effective leadership and initiative:

> I think Susan has changed the focus of the program. I think before she came in the program was … a little more playful, and I think she's turned it into a highly academically oriented program. Not that it wasn't there before, but I think she really helped articulate it … and that was a change. Don't forget, it started with a social integration piece, and now you have full-fledged, two-way bilingual education, with expectations of both languages that are grade-level by fifth grade. And that's been a shift over time.

Effective programs also have leadership from teachers who demonstrate initiative in addressing concerns that have a direct impact on them, such as allocation of instructional time across the two languages. Another quote from Ester de Jong provides an example of how this played out at Barbieri:

> One of the teachers said to me that the nice thing is that when the teachers have a concern, the bilingual program administration listens and tries to support the problem-solving process. So, it goes both ways. Teachers can be frustrated with certain things, for example, the fourth grade in particular has been very tough with the fragmentation [of their day]. [We take] more of a problem-solving approach: What is it that we can do differently? And so several teachers have gone this year to visit programs, and these are programs that we've been working with and visited way back when. So they went back to Salem, they went back to the Amigos program, and talked to the teachers, asking, now how do you do your rotations, and what are you happy with and what are you unhappy with, and just kind of see different models at the upper grades, because a lot of times those [earlier] visits focused on the lower grades. And the issues in the upper grades are different.

Teachers at IAMS expressed a similar sentiment in a general way: "We get together and we discuss new ideas all the time. There is an openness to new ideas. We discuss change all the time. If we feel like we need change, we discuss it and do it." Of course, in both of these cases, the agency shown by the teachers is a direct reflection of the attitude of shared leadership promoted by the principal and, perhaps on a broader level, by the district. At IAMS, for example, there is a district policy of site-based management, meaning that each school has autonomy to make its own decisions related to a number of curricular and instructional matters.

A second area in which individuals in effective programs show agency at the program level is in the acquisition or development of resources, such as instructional materials and assessment measures. As those involved with TWI programs know, appropriate resources in the partner language are frequently difficult to come by, particularly in the upper grades, where content instruction becomes more abstract and complicated. Authentic materials from Latin America or Spain are frequently at a higher language or literacy level than students in TWI classes are used to working with. A quote from a former president of the parent teacher organization (PTO) at Barbieri exemplifies the way that parents and teachers can work together to advocate for better instructional materials in Spanish:

> I used to run the book fairs, and I would have to fight with [the publisher], "I want more Spanish books and higher quality Spanish books," and I basically advocated for the whole town, because this ended up becoming a town-wide thing. To this day, they still can't get them to the book fairs, even though they have a Spanish line. They've had to go to California to get the books … they just don't have them in their warehouses in the Northeast. They've gone to Texas and they've gone to California, and I'm still getting the same junk that they translated…. They're trying to sell books, I want literature. I want good books for them, I don't want junk. I don't want little books about farm animals…. I mean, I have a hard enough time trying to get them to give me a Spanish-English dictionary! There were times the PTO, if we knew they couldn't get us the Spanish-English dictionary, we went and found a source and made sure we had it. Especially after third grade, they really have to have that stuff. We have teachers who'll go to Puerto Rico or other places in the summer and buy materials, and we reimburse them for a lot of stuff….Wherever you have to get the resources, you have to get them. And it's the teachers who really press the issue.

Teachers and administrators at IAMS worked together to develop their own report cards for the students. They were dissatisfied with the district-supplied report cards in terms of the amount of information provided and relevance to bilingual learning environments. Bilingual coordinator Cindy Zucker explained,

The school has developed its own report cards. The district report card is used only in seventh and eighth grades. There are separate report cards for first–third and fourth–sixth [grades]. The report cards focus on the development of skills. The school's report card gives a lot more information. The cards do not use traditional marks. For fourth–sixth, the marks are 1–4, while in first–third, the marks indicate whether a student has mastered a particular skill.

Finally, agency can be demonstrated at the program level through teacher recruitment and professional development. A common lament of TWI administrators is the challenge of finding qualified teachers, particularly those with proficiency in the partner language. This is a core issue, because it has a direct impact on the quality of instruction that can be provided in the partner language and hence on the levels of bilingualism and biliteracy that students in the program are likely to attain.

Minerva Gonzalez of Barbieri articulated her recruitment strategy, stressing that schools have to conduct an active search for the right people rather than waiting for the right people to come to them:

[We recruit] by word of mouth, by going to job fairs, through references, and by asking teachers who may know other educators. Just 2 months ago, I went to a job fair with the human resource director. We went to a minority job fair at Harvard University, and we identified five elementary Hispanic teachers. We have interviewed one of them and we are looking to hire her. We have also had teachers who are teaching abroad and looking to come back to the States. During their break we will invite them back and interview them. Recruitment is about taking advantage of every opportunity, going out and looking for quality teachers, and not just waiting for them to come to you.

Once qualified teachers have been identified, the next challenge is to provide them with appropriate, ongoing, professional development opportunities. Standard professional development opportunities, such as district- or school-initiated inservice sessions, frequently do not relate directly to issues of second language acquisition, the education of language minority students, or the TWI setting. Successful programs ensure that professional development activities match program needs and goals (Lindholm-Leary, 2005) and promote internal professional development through opportunities such as teacher research, teacher study circles (e.g., the Teachers'

Learning Communities at Alicia Chacón [Calderón & Minaya-Rowe, 2003]), and other activities that encourage deep reflection and sharing of ideas.

For example, at Alicia Chacón, teachers are encouraged to share effective instructional approaches that they have developed or been the first to implement. The approach can then be adopted by other teachers and experience broader application.

> It [an instructional approach, such as Language to Literacy] becomes school-wide once it has been properly implemented, the teachers have been trained, and the students show success. When something is witnessed as working, then the staff [who developed it or started working with it first] introduces it to the rest of the staff for approval.

At Key Elementary, the teachers who participated in the teacher-research project found the process to be very informative and useful in a number of ways. As one of the participating teachers reported, the project had the benefit of elevating the status of the teachers and allowing them to take the initiative to choose their own topics and to investigate them deeply, in whatever way was most useful to them and their students.

> Putting my ideas in an organized and analytical manner; working with others; getting guidance; putting my ideas that I've had for a while in a more scientific, serious manner; and for the first time, I think we as teachers were taken seriously. Instead of getting the information from outside, which doesn't apply to what we have, we worked with what we had—it made it more meaningful, more interesting—and you could see the results. It wasn't somebody telling you what to do. You could experiment, you could change things around as needed.

The benefits of encouraging individuals to take ownership of their learning are also found with students at the classroom level in successful TWI programs. The practice of encouraging students to make choices about who they work with, what topics they investigate, or how they go about accomplishing a task is a powerful one that plays out frequently at schools that rely heavily on project-based learning, such as Alicia Chacón and IAMS. The following description of the eighth-grade classroom at Alicia Chacón exemplifies how students can be given all three types of choices simultaneously in a lesson that also incorporates many of the effective instructional strategies discussed earlier, such as integration of language and content, cooperative learning, thematic instruction, and making connections to students' lives. This lesson serves as a vehicle for promoting leadership among the students and for promoting language and literacy development and reinforcing the notion of multilingualism as an asset.

> The students were introduced to a problem-based learning task to relate their knowledge to real life experiences. They were given the following scenario: "Because of Alicia Chacón's unique situation of being an international school, we have been asked to create a new government for Afghanistan." The students were then given examples of various types of governments within their classroom, school, and country. Students were asked to look at the newspaper to see if they could find any information relevant to the project. The front page of the newspaper said, "Afghans to Begin Planning New Government." The students were given time to read the article, and then there was a group discussion about the word alliance and what it meant in the context of both Afghanistan and the school. Through this discussion, the students began to brainstorm on who they would want to work with in small groups to fulfill the objectives of the project. Connections were made to other classes that the students take and the foreign language instruction (in a third language) that they receive. Students were released to the in-class computers, the library, and other resources available in the classroom to begin their work.

Making Public Presentations

A second way that leadership is manifested in effective TWI programs to promote the goals of bilingualism and biliteracy is through the public display of work and ideas, in either speech or writing. At the program level, examples of public presentation can be found at Alicia Chacón, Key, and IAMS, whose teachers frequently present effective instructional strategies and research results at local and national conferences. In fact, the IAMS staff held its own conference and invited teachers from across the district to attend. Other examples were described in vignettes in the previous section: the staff at Barbieri wrote a grant to initiate the TWI program, and the staff at Alicia Chacón present effective instructional approaches to other staff members for potential school-wide adoption.

At the classroom level, encouraging public presentation of work influences language and literacy development in four important ways. First, knowing that a piece of work will be made public or that it will be necessary to speak publicly can provide a strong motivation for students to try hard, to take risks with the language (particularly their second language), and to do their best work. A primary grade teacher at IAMS commented,

> They're eager, so they're on task and they want a good final product, because they know that they're going to share. We give them opportunities to share. It's not just a piece of paper and we collect it and we give them a grade. That's not enough. They need to share it and take it home. Or they're going to have a presentation. That is a motivating factor. Apart from something that you're going to impose on them, it needs to come from them.
>
> I have a class meeting and we rotate—sometimes it's in English and sometimes it's in Spanish. And it's a routine where they congratulate each other for different things, whether it's a safety issue, or helping one another, or using a lot of Spanish. And they really want to do that, so they'll find a way. I give them opportunities to think throughout the week. "Think of somebody that you're going to congratulate." And they'll start going, "How do you say this?" so they are preparing for sharing. So they can do something that recognizes the others. And that really encourages them to take risks with the language.

Second, in a climate that has been carefully designed to be safe and supportive, feedback from peers, the teacher, and others can provide insights on strengths as well as areas for improvement. This, in turn, can foster increasingly higher levels of language and literacy development over time. An example from a fourth-grade classroom at Alicia Chacón demonstrates how peer feedback can target oral presentation skills in particular, promoting public speaking capacity in a project-based lesson that also employs the effective instructional strategies of cooperative learning, language and content integration, and thematic instruction.

> The lesson was an integrated social studies–language arts activity in Spanish. The children read a story in their Spanish literature books about family members who were going to receive their citizenship [that] day. The students then worked on their projects of different countries, each of which represented the country of origin of one of the characters in the story. Each group was to research their country's climate, landform, and significant information about the country for

those who wished to visit it. Once the groups were finished, the presenter of the group read their findings to the rest of the class. Suggestions were given on how to be a better presenter, and questions related to content were also given as feedback.

Third, watching peers present their work orally and in writing can inspire confidence in students, helping them to realize that a seemingly daunting task is actually possible. As one IAMS teacher reported, "They see someone else that they identify with because they are English dominant or whatever is similar to them. They identify with each other. And then they say, 'I can do that too. It's something that's possible, because someone who's close to me has done it.'"

Finally, the self-esteem that emerges from successful presentations and positive peer feedback, as well as from the development that can be noticed when this type of activity is repeated over time, can serve to reinforce students' interest in developing their language and literacy skills to increasingly higher levels in both languages. This may be particularly the case when the presentation is external, beyond the classroom, and students see the real-world value in speaking and writing a language well. For example, all students at IAMS in Grade 2 and above participate in the Young Authors program. This is an activity sponsored by the board of education, in which students write stories and poems to enter in a city-wide contest. Entries are judged, and some are selected for district competition. In an example from Alicia Chacón, a kindergarten student visited some of the older classrooms, where he played his guitar and explained, in Spanish, the various parts of the instrument and how he learned to play. He also welcomed questions from the older students.

Responding to the Needs of Others

A third way that effective TWI programs promote a culture of leadership is by responding to the needs of others through modeling, mentoring, and other forms of peer support, such as second language facilitation. At the program level, this form of leadership can be demonstrated in the way that school leaders, such as the principal, respond to the needs of their staff, or in the ways that peers, such as teachers to teachers or parents to parents, provide support for one another (Lindholm-Leary, 2005). In programs that have team teachers who work together, each providing instruction through one of the program languages, there is a clear need for the teachers to collaborate closely and to communicate regularly about their curriculum, student progress, assessment issues, and so forth. This can be greatly facilitated by the staff responsible for school-level scheduling, as Minerva Gonzalez of Barbieri explains:

> **Interviewer:** Do you think the other two-way teachers feel supported in the school? By the principal?
>
> **Minerva:** Clearly by the principal. A lot of this couldn't happen without the principal. He needed to orchestrate the schedule so that English and Spanish partner teachers would have specials, lunch, and recess together. With the students gone at the same time, we have common planning time, which would not have happened had the principal not agreed to schedule us that way.

Minerva also went on to describe her experiences mentoring new English partner teachers as they joined the program, another way that leaders respond to the needs of others in successful TWI programs. One helpful factor in this mentoring process was the district financial support that was provided for experienced teachers to mentor new teachers. In this way, the district promoted the development of leadership abilities in its teaching staff and encouraged experienced teachers to respond to the needs of new teachers through mentorship. This was particularly crucial in the TWI program; in addition to allowing the new teachers to learn from the experience of the veteran teachers, it promoted stronger connections in curriculum, instruction, and assessment across the two program languages, thus supporting the development of bilingualism and biliteracy among the students.

> We had a year of training, and we also had time to develop materials. When new partner teachers came on board, we became mentors. The town of Framingham offers a mentor program where teachers can take a course on mentoring and receive PDPs [profes-

sional development points] for completing the coursework. Teachers receive a stipend when they mentor someone in their field. Two-way lends itself well to the mentoring program because the best person to mentor a partner teacher is her partner. In my case, I am the only second-grade two-way teacher, so it made sense for me to mentor the new two-way second-grade teacher who was assigned to be my partner. The stipend provides accountability for the mentoring experience, not that I needed that as an incentive. The stipend is the town's way of compensating staff to help integrate and transition new teachers into the system. In two-way, the partnership is like a marriage, as we plan together and do a lot of joint activities together. We'll celebrate holidays, birthdays, and go on field trips together, as well as team teach.

Mentoring of new teachers is common in many educational settings, but in TWI it is particularly important. These teachers face many challenges that are unique to the TWI context, such as promoting bilingualism and biliteracy development for students with varying levels of proficiency in the two languages (Lindholm-Leary, 2005). At IAMS, retired teachers who were founders of the school return every year to provide mentoring for new teachers, to tell them about the school's history and its mission, and to give them a larger context for their work. Additionally, new teachers are paired with veteran teacher-mentors who work with them throughout the year. A second-grade teacher explained, "When I started, I was paired up with … my mentor; we worked together and that was kind of an indoctrination for me as to [what to do] especially as a new teacher. Even if you'd been teaching at another school and come to this school, you need some coaching."

Finally, parents can also demonstrate peer leadership by responding to the needs of other parents in the program and reassuring them when they feel concerned about their child's language development, particularly when the parents do not speak the second language of the program. A former Barbieri PTO president shared her experience:

There's enough of a … friendship system, if you want to call it that, people who've been through it before, almost like mentoring.… I got a call from someone who's going to have a student going into third grade next year, [and I was able to help because] I've been there, I know what it's going to be like. It's parents holding each others' hands.

At the classroom level, peer support is most evident when native speakers are supporting the second language use and development of second language speakers. At Alicia Chacón, the native speakers will remind the second language speakers to use the language of instruction, and this happens during both English and Spanish instructional time. As at other TWI schools, students help each other with translation, particularly during Spanish instructional time. The following example from a fifth-grade Spanish class at Alicia Chacón shows how the students use both languages together effectively to negotiate a complex translation issue involving a homonym in English that does not have a parallel construction in Spanish.

> Rachel: How do you say "meet"?
> Sarah: *Carne* [meat].
> Rachel No, I mean when you meet someone.
> Sarah: *Ver.*
> Rachel: No, that's "to see."
> Sarah: But, that's it.
> Rachel: Shake hands—to meet.
> Sarah: *Conocer.*
> Rachel: Oh!

At IAMS, a teacher addressed the peer translation issue, noting that native language speakers can be supportive in promoting the language development of second language speakers, but that care has to be taken to ensure that the peers are not merely translating everything for the second language learners.

> Most recently I've tried to develop routines where the students have partners and they have opportunities to actually talk and interact in the language, but neither of them can come to me and talk in English if it's Spanish time. If it's something that the student can't say in Spanish, then they would have to go to their partner. Partners can be a problem, because some children are more needy, wanting everything translated, which can wear their partners out. So partners need training, so that one partner doesn't do everything and so that they ask appropriate questions and offer appropriate help. The model keeps the student who needs help from having to ask to have everything translated.

Finally, at Key Elementary, peer support is also provided through peer editing during the writing process. In a second-grade classroom, students went so far as to develop their own guide to peer editing (in Spanish), which the teacher then shared with her English partner teacher, who used it in her class, too. This is an excellent example of the type of useful collaboration across English and Spanish partner teachers that can further the development of students' bilingualism and biliteracy, as discussed earlier. Perhaps more important, it provides an example of how the students were not only able to respond to the needs of other students in a way that enriched their language and literacy development, but were able to respond to the needs of the teachers as well.

Building Consensus and Sharing Leadership

At the program level, a culture of shared leadership is often evident in the ways in which decisions are made about curriculum and instruction. In the four effective TWI programs profiled here, teachers and administrators work together to choose curricular materials and discuss instructional approaches. This type of team approach to leadership is considered advantageous, as it makes the program less vulnerable to fluctuations in personnel, such as the sudden departure of a strong principal or program coordinator (Goldberg, 2001; Lindholm-Leary, 2005).

For example, at Alicia Chacón, at the time of data collection, there was a Kids First Committee that looked at the curriculum and other major aspects of the program and its implementation. One representative from each grade level was a member of this committee, and any major changes in the program or the curriculum were sent through the committee for final approval. This structure allowed for decisions to be made as a school, not on an individual basis.

Cindy Zucker, the bilingual coordinator at IAMS, explained a similar approach used at that school, although IAMS teachers have autonomy to make individual decisions about curriculum and do not have to obtain approval from a school-wide committee:

> The decision-making process is not top down. The decisions are made by the teachers in coordination with the school administration. Specific requests for materials are funneled through an assistant principal, who acts as a liaison between the school and the publishers. The selection of materials is shaped by the resources available, which are often lim-

ited. Teachers have a lot of autonomy in deciding what or how to teach. The implementation of the curriculum, as well as the materials used, are largely decided by the teachers, in conjunction with the administration.

Finally, teachers at Key indicated that they have a strong voice in making important decisions about curriculum and instruction. A primary teacher discussed a recent crossroads about literacy instruction:

> We're definitely at a crossroads figuring out where we're going to take it [literacy instruction] from here. I think we've maxed out on what we're doing now, and we don't know what the answer is, but we know we're ready for a different one. One thing we've considered is possibly having one resource person who spends half a day in one classroom, working with the different groups.... But we're a little worried that that person would become an assistant [who does administrative tasks rather than instruction] and we don't want that. So there are some problems with this kind of team teaching, as well.

It's interesting to note that the school has moved forward with this idea and currently has a resource teacher (e.g., an ESL teacher or a special education teacher) partnering with a classroom teacher to increase access to specialized services and provide a lower student-teacher ratio.

The following example from a primary IAMS classroom demonstrates how shared leadership can occur among students through the use of cooperative groupings, in this case to support vocabulary development through the use of literature circles:

> The students work together in small groups and help each other. One student learns how to spell a word and helps the others. Another concentrates on the meaning and helps the others with that. Another person narrates or retells the story. The person in charge of different aspects rotates, giving all an opportunity to take leadership in different domains and, in so doing, to practice the different skills.

Another example, this one from a fourth-grade classroom at Alicia Chacón, displays many facets of leadership discussed in this chapter and how they can work to promote bilingualism and biliteracy in the students. It involves a 5-day Language to Literacy lesson cycle based on the book *The*

Drinking Gourd. In this example, consensus building and shared leadership are generated through whole-class activities. The activities presented in this lesson cycle are indicative of a balanced literacy approach, incorporate thematic teaching and language and content integration, promote higher order thinking, use cooperative learning, and encourage oral and written language development. In other words, many of the strategies shown to be effective in dual language settings are present here.

> **Teacher:** This method has helped me to get the students interested in reading and connecting it to the writing process. I have been able to see their excitement in the way they participate, and the final products have been pretty awesome.
>
> (Day 1) The students make predictions based on the title and illustrations before reading the book. As students make predictions, I note their predictions on a sheet of chart paper, giving credit to [each student for] their predictions. After the first reading, we check the predictions and place a check mark on whoever had the closest prediction.
>
> (Day 2) I have another chart paper up. On it, I have included the vocabulary that I want the students to focus on (definitions are generated and recorded). Also included on the sheet are "observations." Here, I record the student observations or pertinent comments made during the readings. Again, I always give credit to the participant by recording their name by the comments or observations. I noticed that students are more willing to participate just to get their names on the paper! Then we read the story again. This time we do not necessarily read the whole book through, but students begin to take turns reading and making comments about the reading. For homework, students write a sentence with each vocabulary word.
>
> (Day 3) Some students write their homework sentences on chart paper. The whole class checks them together, and we base it [on whether] the students' sentences are correct or not. (A word the kids liked in this story was *breeches*—not many had heard it before.) I have another chart paper up with the headings "Main Idea" and "Short Summary." After reading and commenting on the story again, I hand students a strip of sentence paper so that each group talks and decides how to write the main idea on their sentence strip. After they are done, we paste it to the chart paper and we discuss each one to decide as a group which sentence best captures the main idea of the story.

We put a check mark next to that sentence. Then we all work together to write the short summary on the chart paper.

(Day 4) Another chart paper sheet goes up with "Point of View." This story served us very well to teach the students why the author wrote the story. (Followed by time to work on Big Book chapters.)

(Day 5) Groups present their own chapter by reading it to the class. Then we laminate the pages and bind the whole book together to keep it in our library.

Conclusion

As shown throughout this chapter through quotes, vignettes, and descriptions of programs and classes, the four programs profiled clearly have strong cultures of leadership that serve to promote the development of bilingualism and biliteracy. To summarize, these are the characteristics of leadership as manifested in these programs:

- **Taking initiative**
  - Shaping program design and implementation, selecting appropriate resources, and identifying priorities for the recruitment and professional development of teachers
  - Promoting agency by allowing students to make choices about who they work with, what topics they investigate, and how they go about accomplishing a given task

- **Making public presentations**
  - Presenting research results and effective instructional strategies at local and national conferences
  - Sharing effective instructional approaches with other staff members for potential broader adoption
  - Encouraging students to present their work to the class to motivate them to do their best work and take risks with their second language

- **Responding to the needs of others**
  - Promoting collaboration or mentoring among teachers, particularly English/Spanish partner teachers or grade-level teams
  - Supporting the use and development of the second language through peer editing and other cooperative activities

- **Building consensus and sharing leadership**
  - Working together, with both teachers and administrators, to choose curricular materials and discuss instructional approaches
  - Using cooperative groupings and whole-class activities that require division of labor or engaging in debate to reach a consensus to complete the task

Chapter 7:
What Does It Look Like?
Intellectualism, Equity,
and Leadership in
Practice

Introduction

In this chapter, we share two approaches developed by veteran teachers in two of the four programs. Both approaches are very strong in that they incorporate all four language skills (listening, speaking, reading, and writing); can be used in both English and Spanish; and promote a variety of strategies, such as cooperative learning, higher order thinking, and language and content integration. Perhaps most important, they do so in a way that also exemplifies the themes discussed in this book—intellectualism, equity, and leadership—at both the program and classroom levels.

The first approach, developed by Ivonne Govea of Key Elementary, was conceived as a teacher-research project. As a first-grade Spanish teacher, Ivonne was concerned about developing the emergent Spanish writing abilities of all of her students, with a particular emphasis on the second language learners (i.e., native English speakers). She developed her approach over the 2 years that she was involved in the teacher-research initiative. The approach has been so successful with both native English speakers and native Spanish speakers that it has been adopted by other primary teachers at Key. Ivonne developed her techniques for Spanish literacy because that is her language of instruction, but the approach is transferable to English as well.

The second approach, developed jointly by Jill Sontag and Cheryl Urow of IAMS, is based on a workshop they attended on note-taking strategies. Jill and Cheryl expanded the concepts of the workshop to include expository report writing as well as note taking, and redesigned the approach to make it more appropriate and useful for students who are developing language and literacy abilities in two languages. Their approach was found to be so effective that it has been adopted school-wide. In addition, Jill and Cheryl have done multiple presentations on the approach at conferences and at school inservice sessions in the Chicago area and elsewhere.

This chapter is devoted to descriptions of these two approaches, written by their creators.

The Development of Spanish Writing Skills in First-Grade TWI Students
By Ivonne Govea, Key Elementary School
Translated from the original Spanish by Elizabeth Howard

Introduction
"¡Sra. Govea, mira! ¡He escrito esta carta para tí! [Mrs. Govea, look! I've written this letter for you!]"* Sabrina told me, proudly smiling as she handed me her letter. I read it and immediately remembered her first writing sample. What a difference! Sabrina is a first grader whose native language is English. Without a doubt, her writing progress provided clear testimony of the success I had in consistently using various strategies designed to develop students' writing abilities.

I'd like to share my experience with other first-grade TWI teachers through this description of my research project, in which I highlight various activities and strategies that help native Spanish speakers as well as native English speakers to develop writing skills in Spanish more efficiently. In my experience at Key School, where the program is designed to teach children a second language through academic content instruction, I observed that the learning of Spanish by the native English speakers continued to be a big challenge, particularly in the domain of writing. Over the years, I tried to help them in the best way possible, using different methods that I varied constantly, in search of a magic bullet that would help me to resolve my frustration at the end of the year, when I was left thinking, "Could I have done more to help this child or that child?" Finally, the opportunity arose to participate in a teacher-research group with my colleagues, and I decided to become part of the group to continue my line of inquiry in a really scientific manner, and to address those unsettling questions that continued to plague me at the end of every school year.

I realize that I have learned a lot from my students over the course of the project—from their hard work, their patience, their consistency, their enthusiasm, and their excellent memory to connect the concepts that they had learned previously, and to sometimes remind me that things that they had learned earlier could be applied today in this lesson. They have been and always will be my inspiration in my classroom.

Activities and Strategies for Developing Spanish Literacy Ability in First Graders

I designed this system of learning using the first-grade Spanish textbook *Lenguage y Comunicación [Language and Communication]* (Santillana). This book has a series of units based on a variety of topics. Each topic introduces a letter of the alphabet, presents a reading passage (short story), and develops vocabulary related to the focal letter. The unit concludes with exercises that involve reading and writing. My system involves the following activities and strategies, which, when applied consistently, resulted in strong Spanish writing outcomes for my students. All of the group activities involved groups that were mixed by native language.

Table 7.1: Activities and Strategies

Activity	Strategies
1. Introduce the focal letter.	• Pronounce the letter (model the sound). • Show how the letter is formed (capital and lower case).
2. Introduce the poster for the unit.	• Solicit and respond to questions about the poster. • Present the poster along with its characters and/or subjects and describe them.

Table 7.1: Activities and Strategies	
Activity	**Strategies**
3. Introduce the vocabulary.	• Present the vocabulary cards. These will be used for daily practice. • Count the syllables in each word. • Discuss the meaning of the target vocabulary and solicit additional vocabulary items that begin with the focal letter. • Group the words by the initial syllable. • Practice spelling the words. • Practice learning the vocabulary in partner dyads through dictation and self-check.
4. Read the story in the unit.	• Direct choral group reading. • Direct individual reading. • Reinforce the rules of punctuation and capitalization by noting their use in the story. • Analyze the components of the sentences in the story (subject-verb-complement).

5. Present the workbook for the unit, e.g., "My book of Mm," and teach the children how to work through it.	• Use the overhead projector to demonstrate the activities needed to complete the workbook (primarily the first two letters). The workbook consists of the following:
	
	  • A short story that introduces the unit—here the students had to circle all of the capital letters.
	
	  • A page that introduces the vocabulary words for the unit (with accompanying pictures)—here the students had to count and separate the syllables of each word.
	
	  • A page where students have to group the vocabulary words based on their initial syllable.
	
	  • Two to three pages with writing exercises where students have to finish writing vocabulary words, pair or relate words, complete sentences, etc.

Table 7.1: Activities and Strategies	
Activity	**Strategies**
6. Facilitate the cooperative activity of creating sentences out of the vocabulary for the unit.	• Present a set of cards that is based on the vocabulary for the unit and includes nouns, pronouns, articles, verbs, prepositions, and conjunctions. • Classify the vocabulary cards by categories: nouns or names (people, animals, or things), actions or verbs, and other words that help in sentence formation (includes the components of the predicate or the complement, as well as prepositions, conjunctions, articles, etc.). • Facilitate the active participation of each group to manipulate the cards to form a single sentence. • Check the accuracy of each group's sentence in terms of grammar, mechanics, and meaning. • Approve the sentence if it is accurate or encourage further work if it is not. • Have each student in the group write the sentence on a piece of paper once it has been approved. • Have each group repeat the process until time is up. • Count the total number of sentences written by each group.
7. Evaluate the learning of vocabulary from the unit.	• Review the vocabulary in groups, paying particular attention to spelling. • Practice vocabulary in pairs through dictation and self-checking. • Dictate the vocabulary words to the entire class and have the students correct their own paper.
8. Collect the writing samples.	• Be flexible with regard to topic, and allow for some student choice. Broadly, topics can relate to the unit of study, an important event in the school, a holiday, a season, etc. • Have students write independently but let them interact and ask each other for assistance as they write.
9. Evaluate and analyze the writing samples.	• Use the writing rubric.

The Effects of Heterogeneous Grouping

Through my observations, I was able to see the effects of the heterogeneous grouping for the cooperative activities. For example, when the students were working in groups, making sentences by manipulating the vocabulary cards, it was interesting to see how they interacted to form each sentence—correcting one another, noticing if the sentence started with a capital letter, checking for subject-verb agreement or gender or number agreement. To do this, they read each sentence aloud to see if it made sense or not. In this activity, I could see how the native Spanish speakers strongly supported the construction of the sentences, primarily in the first few months, when they were the primary leaders of group discussions. By the end of the project, the participation of the two native language groups was balanced to about 50% contribution by each group. This gave me an indication of the success of the interactions in the heterogeneous groups.

In the future, I plan to continue the use of small, heterogeneous cooperative groups. I found that working in mixed groups allowed the native English speakers to be exposed to a more authentic working environment. Perhaps more important, this activity truly elevated the status of the native Spanish speakers, as they were clearly the experts who were able to confirm or challenge the grammatical accuracy of the sentences that the groups were formulating in activity 6.

Writing Samples

Sometimes the writing samples related directly to the topic of the unit, while other times they referred to the season—holidays like Mother's Day or the Day of Friendship—or they simply reflected the individual musings of the students after having engaged in a field trip or a school activity that they enjoyed. To score the writing samples, I used the writing rubric developed by the partial immersion program in Arlington Public Schools (www.cal.org/twi/rubrics) as a point of departure and made some adjustments to it that aligned it to the specific considerations of my study. The skills that I scored are as follows:

- Length: number of sentences
- Composition
- Sentence formation

- Usage/agreement
  - Correct use of nouns in both singular and plural
  - Correct use of gender
  - Recognition of the direct relationship between article and noun
- Mechanics
  - Spelling
  - Capitalization
  - Punctuation

Findings

At the start of the study, the majority of the students (both native English speakers and native Spanish speakers) exhibited difficulty writing correct, simple sentences that expressed a complete idea. Their errors generally consisted of the omission of some of the components of the sentence. To overcome these difficulties, I worked intensively on the identification of nouns or names, actions or verbs, and complements of the sentence through sentence formation activities based on the vocabulary from the thematic unit. I also encouraged the students to analyze the sentences grammatically. To do this, I created sets of three cards, each in a different color, and each with the name of one of the sentence components (noun/name, action/verb, or complement) on it. I wrote sentences on the board, and the students were responsible for copying the sentence and then placing the right card under each corresponding part of the sentence.

Over time, I saw that the native English speakers were best able to formulate sentences when they worked with vocabulary from a thematic unit that they were already familiar with. Moreover, the repetitive practice in using content vocabulary to formulate sentences served to strengthen skills in applying gram-matical rules when writing in Spanish. This showed me that it's important to capitalize on thematic content, such as "my family," "my friends," and so forth. The children use vocabulary related to these themes on a daily basis, and it was possible to take advantage of this familiarity when teaching writing and reinforcing the rules of accentuation, capitalization, gender and number agreement, verb conjugation, etc. This possibility is further enriched when the students work in heterogeneous groups with both native English speakers and native Spanish speakers.

The Impact of My Research on My Instruction

My study allowed me to confirm that the activities and strategies that I was using were effective in developing the Spanish writing skills of my native Spanish speakers and, particularly, my native English speakers. I found that consistent use of the same learning system through various units of instruction was crucial. Another important and enriching strategy was putting students in small, heterogeneous groups and giving them the opportunity to interact with one another. I also found that videotaping the students during the activities allowed me to discover many smaller details in their processes of learning to write in Spanish, so this is something that I continue to do.

At the end of the year, I found satisfaction in noting that my focus on the development of writing had allowed me to achieve several objectives with my students:

- Developing their ability to form letters and words with fluency and clarity
- Promoting their desire to communicate in writing
- Developing their knowledge and understanding of sound-symbol correspondence
- Stimulating the development of legibility, clarity, order, and precision in their written expression
- Stimulating their ability to evaluate their own writing

Fascinating Facts and Remarkable Reports: An Approach to Note Taking and Expository Writing for Two-Way Immersion Classrooms

**By Jill Sontag, Inter-American Magnet School
and Cheryl Urow, Illinois Resource Center**

Setting the Context

We both began our teaching careers at the Inter-American Magnet School (IAMS) in Chicago. Inter-American is the oldest TWI program in the Midwest and has served as a model program for other TWI programs throughout the country. Part of what makes Inter-American a model program is the culture of empowerment in the school. Teachers are involved in every decision. The administration regularly consults with teachers and doors are open to any issue or concern that requires discussion. Collaboration among teachers is actively fostered, and teachers are encouraged to develop units and lessons based on the strengths and needs of students. It is common to hear discussions about teaching in the hallways and in the staff dining room. Many grade-level teams hold weekly afterschool meetings on their own time to reflect upon their practices and plan units and lessons together. In addition, there is a strong parent presence in the school. Parents are seen changing bulletin board displays in the hallways, disseminating information in the office, tutoring children in the classrooms, and sharing their expertise in lessons and units of study. It was in this nurturing environment—where teachers, students, and parents all thrived—that we began teaching and where we were able to take the professional chances that allowed us to create some innovative units of study for our classrooms.

Within this context of extreme professionalism at Inter-American, teachers share the high expectations they have for themselves, their colleagues, and their students. We soon learned from other teachers about grants for building classroom libraries and classes to take for improving our teaching. As novice teachers, we wrote and received small grants from the Rochelle Lee Foundation to buy books in Spanish and English to build well-balanced bilingual classroom libraries. As a stipulation for receiving the grant monies, recipients had to attend a number of workshops offered by the foundation and present workshops of their own at local or national conferences. During one of the workshops we attended, we were introduced to the idea of Fascinating Facts. While reading nonfiction books, we were told to jot down interesting facts—one per sticky note. We took this strategy for reading nonfiction and adapted it to the TWI setting at Inter-American.

TWI teachers do not have a lot of time. We have to teach all of the content that general education teachers are required to teach plus two language arts classes. And to top it off, we are always teaching in someone's second language. For that reason, TWI teachers are always looking for ways to better integrate content and literacy instruction and for ways of making content comprehensible yet challenging for all learners. To help accomplish these multiple challenging goals, we had already created and implemented many hands-on activities in our classrooms. For example, at the time we went to the Fascinating Facts workshop, Jill's second-grade class was raising four different kinds of insects (mealworms, wax worms, milkweed bugs, and butterflies), which they took care of in different grouping configurations. Each student cared for his or her own mealworms. Pairs took care of the wax worms. Each table of four or five children set up milkweed bug habitats, and the whole class looked after the butterflies. They kept track of the care of each one with schedules and used a variety of calendars, journals, and charts to record hypotheses and observations—all in Spanish. A running list of key vocabulary in Spanish was kept on display for the class at all times for children to use as reminders and references during both discussion and writing times.

Using a Hands-On Approach to Generate Interest

While Jill's class was studying insects, Cheryl had ordered crayfish for her third graders to care for and study. With the idea of Fascinating Facts in mind, Cheryl went back to her classroom to prepare her students for the arrival of the crayfish. Knowing that nonfiction reading materials at a third-grade reading level would not be readily available in Spanish, Cheryl planned to begin the crayfish unit in Spanish but move the students to English to look for fascinating facts. She also planned to integrate Spanish literacy into the unit, both by having students document their observations and by having them write narratives in Spanish about the arrival of the crayfish from the point of view of the crayfish.

Cheryl began the unit by introducing the vocabulary that the students would need to care for the crayfish and study their behaviors and physical characteristics. She told the students, in Spanish, that she would be bringing in a live animal the next day. It was their job to guess the identity of the animal through a series of yes/no questions. Cheryl gave the students a few minutes to talk in their small groups—groups of four or five mixed heterogeneously—to come up with questions in Spanish. Before beginning the questioning, Cheryl reminded the students of language structures that would be useful for asking yes/no questions in Spanish. For example, "*¿Necesita...?* [Does it need ... ?]" is a good way to begin a question in Spanish. As students asked questions, Cheryl posted only the correct answers on chart paper. While she and the students spoke only Spanish, the English equivalents of the "yes" answers were also posted on the paper. This chart paper was to serve as a resource to help students maintain the target language and to transfer their knowledge from one language to the other.

The questions the students asked allowed Cheryl to introduce the vocabulary she knew they would need. For example, if a student asked, "*¿Vive en el agua?* [Does it live in water?],*" Cheryl was able to respond, "*Si, vive en agua dulce* [Yes, it lives in fresh water]." Few third graders would have the sophistication to ask if an animal lived in salt or fresh water, but their simple question opened the door for Cheryl to introduce the language they needed to figure out the secret animal. As students asked more and more questions, the level of discussion within each cooperative group increased. Each person in the group was required to ask one question in Spanish before anyone in the group could ask a second question. This strategy encouraged a great deal of discussion in the small groups and a good deal of peer-to-peer language teaching and language learning. Also, introducing a topic of high interest in the partner language—a live animal in the classroom!—and intimately tying the study of this high-interest subject to the partner language greatly increased the status and importance of the partner language in the classroom.

Transitioning From Hands-On to Literacy, From Spanish to English

The crayfish arrived in Cheryl's class, and the insects in Jill's class prospered. The children worked excitedly in their respective classrooms and, as they did, generated more and more questions. As a segue for moving from the hands-on activity to the literacy component, we both kept track of our students' questions and wrote them down in two lists. We did not, at first, explain the organizational or thematic rationale behind either of the lists. After the students had spent several days observing, caring for, and keeping logs on the animals, we asked them to look at the two lists of questions and think about what each list represented. In Cheryl's room, for example, list A had questions like, "*¿Un langostino puede comer una cucaracha?* [Can a crayfish eat a cockroach?]"; List B included questions like, "*¿De que color son los huevos de un langostino?* [What color are crayfish eggs?]." After allowing the students to discuss the issue in their small groups, Cheryl took answers from the students. Generally, the children were able to discern that the questions in list A could be answered through an experiment they could do in class, while the questions in list B could best be answered through research. It was at this point that the unit became multidisciplinary and bilingual.

Cheryl continued with the "experiment" questions in Spanish. In science class, students reviewed the elements of the scientific process. After choosing a question from the list or coming up with a new one, pairs of students wrote up a description of their experiment, the materials they needed, and their hypothesis. Again, because the students came up with the experiments that they would conduct, they were highly motivated to do the work and to maintain the partner language—both during oral discussion and during the literacy portion. Students were also motivated to supply all the needed materials. One student eagerly told Cheryl that she had cockroaches at her house and would be able to bring them for a particular experiment. Students then conducted their experiments, then wrote detailed observations of the experiments and the results.

But that still left all the questions in list B, those that were best answered through research. It was clear to both of us that there was potential for using the children's natural motivation and curiosity stemming from these units to teach research skills in an authentic way, and that the Fascinating Facts strategy would work well within a research unit for several reasons. First, this strategy encouraged students to think about what they were reading. Second, the small area of the sticky note encouraged students to paraphrase or use key words rather than copying verbatim from the text. Finally, it was a strategy that could be used with reading materials at a variety of reading levels—a necessity in any classroom, but particularly in a TWI setting where many students are at varying levels of second language proficiency as well as reading ability. By integrating the Fascinating Facts strategy into a unit on research, students could find the answers to their own questions while developing a new set of reading and writing skills. Plus, we would be introducing them to the tools needed to become independent learners in two languages. Again, since most resources available for children on these topics were in English, we decided to make research the English component of our integrated units.

We wanted the transition from studying insects and crayfish in Spanish to studying them in English to be a conscious one. To facilitate this move and to get the students to think about transferring their knowledge from one language to another, we began the research portion by asking the students to write in English everything they already knew about their animals (crayfish in third grade, insects in second grade)—one fact per sticky note. The bilingual vocabulary list generated in the first activity in third grade was an important transitional tool for the third graders during this activity. This brainstorming of everything they already knew about their subject served as a way to get the students to begin thinking in English and introduced them to the Fascinating Facts procedure. Each student was given a file folder on which to affix the sticky notes, which would be used later.

Once these first fascinating facts were generated, we realized that we now had to teach the children how to do research. Because they were second and third graders, we knew that we had to start at the very beginning of the research process. We also recognized that we would have to scaffold the process by modeling, thinking aloud, and giving the children time to practice each step along the way. We began with a general whole-class brainstorm based on the question, "Where do we get information?" followed by the more specific brainstorm, "How do we get information from books?" We reminded the students about all the questions they had generated and how they had suggested that we could best find the answers to these questions through research. We asked the children, "Where could we get the answers to these questions?" Again, students were encouraged to talk in their cooperative groups before suggesting an answer. Students offered such answers as books, the Internet, the zookeeper, and Mom as sources of information. We recorded those answers on a graphic organizer on a piece of chart paper.

We then focused specifically on how to find information in books. Students talked in their small groups and then suggested such sources as pictures, the table of contents, and the words. These answers were posted on another piece of chart paper. We each took this opportunity to introduce some of the research tools we would be discussing, such as the index, the table of contents, and captions. To familiarize students with these elements of nonfiction text, we would hold games such as index races, where, using the index, children had to find the topic we called out and then hold up the book turned to the correct page as soon as they found it. Other variations included table of contents races and glossary races, as well as the general "find information on a given topic any way you can." This last approach gives a good idea of how advanced students' techniques are for finding information. For example, students who use the index to find that information are using a more sophisticated method than those who are randomly paging through the book.

Once the children had gained some hands-on experience with both non-fiction books and their subjects, they refocused on the questions they had generated. Before beginning the research, Jill decided to put her second-grade students in small groups. She had each student list the top 10 insects they were most interested in studying. She was then able to put them into groups of three according to their areas of interest, while balancing each group academically, linguistically, and socially. In Cheryl's third-grade class, each child was responsible for researching crayfish individually.

Teaching the Fascinating Facts Strategy

The next step of the process was to teach the Fascinating Facts strategy. First, we modeled the process involved in taking notes. We started by using the index to find a page that held information on the subject to be researched, and then we read a portion aloud. We then modeled our own thinking process by using phrases such as, "What I think this is saying is …" or "That sounds to me like …" and proceeded to write our thoughts on a sticky note. After modeling the read-aloud/think-aloud/paraphrase process several times, the teacher invited the students to paraphrase what she read aloud. This process was likewise repeated several times, and students were invited to discuss their ideas with partners or small groups before offering a paraphrased version of the text.

This teacher-modeling phase presents a number of important teachable moments. First, it was during this phase that we had the opportunity to clarify what constitutes a fascinating fact. Specifically, students don't need to write something down if they know the fact already. Students need to be reminded that they already know a lot about the subject they are studying, thanks to the hands-on portion of the unit, and they only need to focus on new information. Second, this is the opportunity to teach metacognitive strategies. We took the opportunity to model what to do when you don't understand a particularly difficult passage that you've just read, using such phrases as, "I really don't understand what I just read" or "I understood the part about … but not the part about.…" We think students should be taught the skills of skimming and scanning for information and how to recognize when it is appropriate to skip or reread portions of the text. Throughout this modeling phase, we continued to reinforce the use of research tools like the index, table of contents, and captions. Finally, it was also important at this stage to demonstrate how much the students already knew from studying the subject in Spanish, and how they could use what they had learned in one language to facilitate their learning in the other language. For example, they would likely be exposed to many cognates, and this was a great opportunity to explicitly teach what cognates are and how to use them. In Cheryl's third-grade classroom, for example, the students began a cognate wall that included words like pincers, crustacean, and antenna.

In second grade, this modeling phase, where the teacher read aloud and the students took notes, took several days. In third grade, however, the students were ready to begin taking notes on their own after a single introductory modeling lesson. Both second- and third-grade students spent about a week doing research on their own. The second graders worked in small groups, as detailed below, and the third graders worked independently. However, while each third grader had to collect his or her own notes, students were encouraged to read and take notes in pairs, to discuss their new and fascinating information with peers, and to share resources. In addition, Cheryl provided the third graders with several mini-lessons (such as the one on cognates) during their week of independent note taking.

In second grade, students worked in groups and collected their notes in group folders. In addition, in some groups they divided up the work according to their strengths and needs. For example, in one group of three, one student read aloud to the other two, who orally paraphrased the information back to the reader. The reader then wrote what they said, one fact at a time, on sticky notes, and the other two took turns putting them in the folder. Because students were working in small groups, Jill had the opportunity to observe and take notes on student work and monitor it accordingly. Jill was careful to ensure that there was a wide variety of reading material, at a variety of reading levels, thus enabling all students to take the role of reader or writer at some time during the research phase.

Both of us, through a combination of visits to a public library, the school library, and through funds from additional grants that we pursued, brought in many English books about the students' topics at a variety of reading levels. It is important to have as many texts at as many levels as possible so that each student can participate fully in the process. Occasional collaboration with the school's computer teacher allowed the students to take notes from Internet resources in school, and those who had Internet access at home voluntarily continued the work at home.

Organizing Fascinating Facts Through Macro-Organization and Micro-Organization

Once enough notes were collected by each group or individual, we began to teach students how to organize them. This step involved analyzing and classifying information through a process that Cheryl named "macro-organization." We each brought our class together as a group and asked for volunteers to read some interesting facts aloud. As each fact was read, we decided together with the class whether it belonged with others that had been shared or if it should begin a new column. This macro-organization generates a lot of natural debate and is a great place to practice and develop oral language skills. In particular, it provides a wonderful opportunity for a teacher to introduce the language structures that go along with persuasion and debate. The teacher can model and post such phrases as, "I disagree. I think that …" or "I agree with _____ because _____." This may even serve as a starting point later for a more formal lesson on writing persuasive essays or participating in a debate.

As more and more facts were shared and categorized, the class assigned category names to each column. For the second-grade insect unit, the whole class came up with five categories: food, behavior, life cycle, habitat, and extra (for notes that were interesting but miscellaneous). In third grade, students came up with categories such as food, enemies, and babies (which, with help from Cheryl, was renamed reproduction).

Once this macro-organization was modeled, students returned to their own notes to organize them on a large piece of construction paper. In second grade, the students copied and used the categories they had created together as a class. In third grade, the class-generated categories served only as a model. During this phase, we reminded students to bring in their fascinating facts from the very first activity in English, when they wrote down everything they already knew about the animals they were studying from the hands-on activities they had done earlier in Spanish. It is important for students to understand that research includes information that is learned through direct observation or experimentation. Each student or group of students then redistributed their own sticky notes according to the categories that had been established. In second grade, where students were working in small groups, this categorization of the stickies allowed the students to practice the oral language skills of debate and persuasion in a small-group setting.

When the macro-organization was complete, the students were ready to organize the notes within each individual column, a process that Cheryl named "micro-organization." Here we modeled how to order information in a logical sequence. In both classes, we began this part by using the organized notes from one group or one student. We read through all the notes within a specific column, and then asked the students which note should go first. In third grade, it was only necessary to model this process with the notes from a single category, as students quickly caught on to the idea. In second grade, however, Jill modeled the process repeatedly with several categories. In both cases, quite a bit of discussion ensued, reinforcing the idea that this would be a great place to focus on the language of polite debate and persuasion. Children had varying opinions on how to organize information and noted that different categories lent themselves to different forms of organization, such as chronological ordering for information on the life cycle versus ordering information from the general to the specific in the behavior category.

When it seemed the whole class understood how to organize a column, each second-grade group chose a single category to rearrange in a physical sequence. This was a way of adapting the activity to second grade, and it also helped the students to see that researchers do not always use all of the information they collect. In third grade, students organized the information in all of their categories. During this phase, the students often noticed that they were missing information. For example, when the second-grade notes in the life cycle category for the ladybug were organized chronologically, one group realized that they were missing a lot of information on the pupa stage, while they had a lot of sticky notes on the larva and adult stages. The students then initiated the idea of returning to the books to look for the missing information.

From Fascinating Facts to Remarkable Reports

When the students had finished the micro-organization stage, they had essentially constructed paragraphs by physically manipulating their sticky notes. They were therefore ready to transfer these notes to paper in the form of written paragraphs. In second grade, Jill modeled this transition with one of the unused categories, showing how the names of the categories help them come up with topic sentences, such as "There are three important stages in the life cycle of a lady bug." In third grade, Cheryl modeled paragraph writing by using the notes of one of the more hesitant writers. The class worked together to write the first paragraph using the student's micro-organized notes. This accomplished the dual objectives of modeling the procedure for the whole class while scaffolding the process for a struggling writer in an efficient and respectful way.

One of the first lessons we teach during this Writing Together activity is the idea of an opening sentence. Working together, and with some guidance from us, the students came up with an opening sentence for the report. We also had the opportunity to model the thought process that goes into creating an opening sentence: "What would attract a reader? Who is my audience? What am I writing about?" Once an opening sentence was written, the fascinating facts were made into complete sentences. Transition words were added. Compound sentences were created. In addition, we had the opportunity to review such writing conventions as indentation, capitalization, and punctuation. Once this first paragraph was written, it served as a model for students. In addition, the reluctant third-grade writer whose notes were used as the point of departure for the paragraph was able to copy this group-written paragraph and was now ahead of the rest of class and more highly motivated to continue.

One important characteristic of this unit is that as the students move through it, they become increasingly invested in their work. Much of the revisiting of the categories, note taking, and reworking of the final report is student driven. Similarly, once the reports are finished, the children decide what to do with them. In the past, the second grade has used them as articles in an insect newspaper they published. Third graders went on crayfish visits around the school and presented their findings to different classes. Another year, they used their facts to create many different games as part of a crayfish carnival.

Extensions of This Approach

In the last few years, teachers at the school have chosen to extend this research technique to several grades through our school-wide social studies curriculum of the Americas, in which each grade does an extended integrated unit based on different peoples indigenous to the Americas. First graders study the Native Americans of the United States, second graders study the Tainos of the Caribbean, third graders study the Incas of South America, fourth graders study the Mayas, fifth graders study the Aztecs, and sixth graders study a combination of all of these with the addition of the African experience in the Americas. For the majority of our Latino and African American students, the end result is that they are researching their heritage at one point or another. Naturally, parents make regular visits to classrooms to share aspects of their culture, and teachers work hard to bring in community members, politicians, authors, artists, and musicians from these cultures. The guests have shown instruments and played music; done art projects such as weaving, pottery, and feather work; told stories about themselves; taught classes in indigenous languages such as Quechua or Quiché; brought in traditional foods or dishes; talked about their cosmologies and historical perspectives; and empowered students to take some form of action to help make the world a more equitable place.

These hands-on and personal experiences have encouraged the students to ask questions and want to learn more. The students move from the hands-on and personal to seeking a deeper understanding through research. And the wide breadth of the subjects being studied requires the students to use all of their skills—listening, speaking, reading, and writing—in both languages.

Conclusion

As summarized in Table 7.2 below, both of the instructional approaches described in this chapter are strong on a number of dimensions: They exemplify the three central themes discussed in this book—intellectualism, equity, and leadership—as well as a number of well-documented instructional strategies for dual language classrooms; they are also very flexible in that they can be used with a variety of grade levels, for various subjects, and in English or Spanish.

Table 7.2: Summary of Approaches for Developing Bilingualism and Biliteracy

	Promoting Writing Development: Ivonne Govea	Fascinating Facts and Remarkable Reports: Jill Sontag and Cheryl Urow
Intellectualism at the program level	Ivonne developed the approach through her participation in a 2-year teacher-research project.	Jill and Cheryl took an idea from a mainstream literacy workshop and modified it for TWI, expanding it considerably to promote oral and written language development in both English and Spanish.
Intellectualism at the classroom level	Students work in cooperative groups to form their own sentences (activity 6). The sentence-creation task involves a great deal of discussion and debate. Many activities promote higher order thinking, in particular the sentence-creation and writing tasks.	Students work frequently in different cooperative groupings and rely on one another for exchange of information and opinions. The curriculum is challenging and largely student centered. Many activities promote higher order thinking.
Equity at the program level	The approach was developed in the context of the program at Key, where the language of instruction alternates on a half-day basis and content areas are taught exclusively in one language or the other. As a result, until recently, Spanish language arts was taught solely through the content areas, and Ivonne's approach was among the pioneering efforts to develop a dedicated block of Spanish language arts instruction. By utilizing an integrated approach to develop listening, speaking, reading, and writing abilities in Spanish, Ivonne is able to do this in an effective and efficient manner.	This approach came out of a grant that Cheryl and Jill wrote because of a need for literacy materials in their classrooms, particularly in Spanish. The school has adopted the practice, and teachers at all grade levels now use it to teach social studies units focusing on various Latino and Afro-Latino/African American cultures.

Table 7.2: Summary of Approaches for Developing Bilingualism and Biliteracy

	Promoting Writing Development: Ivonne Govea	Fascinating Facts and Remarkable Reports: Jill Sontag and Cheryl Urow
Equity at the classroom level	This approach does a lot to promote the status of the Spanish language and the native Spanish speakers. The activities promote strong language and literacy abilities in Spanish, which helps students use the language more in the classroom. Also, the native Spanish speakers have elevated status during the sentence-construction task in particular, because of their intuitive knowledge of Spanish grammar—they become the experts in determining appropriate agreement, placement, vocabulary choice, and so forth. Specific content may have multicultural themes.	The approach was designed by Cheryl and Jill to be used in TWI settings in particular, and to strengthen language and literacy skills in both English and Spanish through the development of a variety of activities related to a common content theme. The approach therefore allows all students an opportunity to work in their native language and their second language and to feel simultaneously supported and challenged as a result. Specific content may have multicultural themes.
Leadership at the program level	The approach has been adopted by other primary teachers in the program. Ivonne is now teaching fifth grade and is working to expand the approach for the upper grades and to encourage systematicity program-wide.	Developed in response to a workshop Jill and Cheryl attended after writing a grant for materials, their approach was eventually adopted program-wide. Jill and Cheryl also have presented the approach at various conferences and workshops.
Leadership at the classroom level	Students sometimes have choice of writing topics; students provide peer support to each other during various tasks, particularly the sentence-construction task.	Students have a great deal of choice in their areas of investigation; students take turns in different roles within cooperative groupings.
Effective instructional strategies	Cooperative learning, sheltered instruction, higher order thinking, multiple modes of instruction, thematic instruction, language and content integration	Cooperative learning, sheltered instruction, higher order thinking, multiple modes of instruction, thematic instruction, language and content integration

Chapter 8:
Putting It All Together

Through examples drawn from four highly effective programs, we have discussed the importance of three cultures in promoting bilingualism and biliteracy development through TWI education. First, a culture of **intellectualism** involves having a commitment to ongoing learning, encouraging collaboration and the exchange of ideas, fostering independence, and promoting higher order thinking. Second, a culture of **equity** entails valuing and protecting time for the partner language and its associated culture(s), promoting bilingualism for students with special needs, balancing the needs of native English speakers and native Spanish speakers, and fostering an appreciation for multiculturalism. Finally, a culture of **leadership** promotes behaviors such as taking initiative, public presentation, responding to the needs of others, and consensus building and shared leadership.

The four programs profiled in this book provide strong examples of how the cultures of intellectualism, equity, and leadership can play out in practice in TWI programs and classrooms. In addition, these programs all share an approach to biliteracy development that is characterized by a number of key instructional strategies known to be essential for enriched language education environments (Calderón & Minaya-Rowe, 2003; Cloud et al., 2000; Freeman et al., 2005; Soltero, 2004). Specifically, as we discussed in chapter 2, teachers in these programs employ a balanced approach to literacy instruction that includes both direct skills instruction and meaning-making activities. Language instruction takes place both through explicit language arts instruction (which sometimes includes targeted ESL and SSL instruction) and through thematic content area instruction that integrates language objectives with content objectives. Throughout these lessons, teachers rely on a number of sheltered instruction strategies, such as the use of visual aids, realia, and graphic organizers; appropriate modeling and scaffolding of both content and language concepts; and attention to multiple modalities of learning. To promote rich and extensive language input and output, activities are largely student centered, employing cooperative learning techniques and differentiated instruction, frequently within a framework of project-based learning. Effective teachers in these programs capitalize on the incipient bilingualism of their students to promote metalinguistic awareness and cross-linguistic connections, such as through the study of cognates. Finally, teachers in all four programs view assessment as a crucial aspect of instruction and therefore use formative assessment to guide their instruction for all students.

Although the four schools share a commitment to these essential instructional techniques and to the core characteristics and goals of TWI (Howard & Christian, 2002), they have very different program models. Two employ a Spanish-dominant (80/20 or 80/10/10) model, one uses a 50/50 model, and one has a differentiated model intended to develop foundational math and literacy skills in each student's native language in the primary grades. The programs also vary in the language used for initial literacy instruction (Spanish only, both English and the partner language simultaneously, or each student in his or her native language) and in their use of targeted ESL/SSL support by a classroom teacher or other staff member in homogenous language groups.

As we discussed in chapter 3, these program model decisions can have an impact on student outcomes. Specifically, based on the Key findings reported here and on other research on this topic (Lindholm-Leary & Howard, in press), it appears that the 50/50 model generally leads to lower Spanish proficiency outcomes than other program models. Similarly, Barbieri's differentiated model, while effective in many ways, generally produced lower-than-average Spanish proficiency outcomes for the native English speakers. It also placed undue pressure on the upper elementary teachers to quickly elevate the Spanish proficiency of the native English speakers to allow them to keep pace with their native-Spanish-speaking peers, particularly while engaged with more complex and abstract academic work. In recent years, this challenge has been compounded by the additional pressures related to English standardized achievement testing at the upper elementary level. Both programs are aware of these implications of their program model decisions and are now making instructional (Key) or programmatic (Barbieri) changes to address them.

Conversely, the mean third-grade English language and literacy performance of Alicia Chacón students was sometimes lower than study averages, while mean performance in later grades was consistently as high as or higher than study means. Again, this phenomenon is supported by other research that indicates that in the early elementary grades, students in 90/10 or other partner-language-dominant models sometimes demonstrate lower levels of English achievement than students in other programs, but that by the upper elementary grades, they reach comparable or higher levels (Lindholm-Leary & Howard, in press). Our conversations with practitioners in the field suggest that this potential delay in early English outcomes is a disincentive for programs to employ the 90/10 model, particularly in the current high-stakes testing atmosphere made acute by the demands of the federal No Child Left Behind Act. Alicia Chacón is fortunate that Texas has a Spanish version of the state standardized achievement test that schools are allowed to use for accountability purposes. If other states provided this type of testing flexibility, we believe that more TWI programs would be inclined to implement Spanish-dominant approaches, particularly given the higher levels of Spanish they seem to promote without any long-term sacrifice to English language development for either native language group.

Despite these variations in outcomes, it is still fair to say that all four schools have succeeded in promoting bilingualism and biliteracy development for all of their students. Chapter 3 provided ample evidence of the impressive outcomes of both native Spanish speakers and native English speakers relative to each other, to study means, to district and state comparison groups, and to standardized test norms. As research on other TWI programs has shown to be the case (Howard, Sugarman, et al., 2003), our research findings from these four programs indicate a native language effect, with native speakers frequently outperforming second language learners. Finally, the data from these four programs support earlier findings that there appear to be different patterns of development for native English speakers and native Spanish speakers. Native Spanish speakers tend to become more balanced bilinguals than native English speakers, who tend to score consistently higher in English than in Spanish (Howard, Sugarman, et al., 2003).

In chapter 4, we discussed how a culture of intellectualism is manifested at the program and classroom levels. Both adults and students are supported in ongoing learning, reflection, and the use of higher order thinking skills to pursue ideas deeply. This involves taking risks and making mistakes in a supportive and encouraging atmosphere where the development of lifelong skills is valued. Both adults and children also collaborate on a regular basis: teachers through joint planning and learning about each others' practices, and students through opportunities to share during group discussions and through hands-on projects. In this way, both teachers and students have opportunities to learn from one another in various contexts. While we cannot assume a causal relationship between the existence of this type of collaboration and the high outcomes discussed in chapter 3, the fact that effective programs use these collaborative activities supports the sociocultural theory of learning (Rogoff et al., 1996; Tharp & Gallimore, 1988; Vygotsky, 1978).

Creating a culture of equity within a TWI program, as discussed in chapter 5, runs counter to the normative discourse in American society (Freeman, 1998), but it is important for both pedagogical and social reasons to resist the overwhelming power of English as the dominant language in the United States. Pedagogically, it is important to provide enough instructional time through the partner language for students to develop proficiency in that language (Howard, Sugarman, et al., 2003; Lindholm-Leary, 2001; Lindholm-Leary & Howard, in press). Socially, many teachers and parents have reflected on the alienation they felt as linguistic or ethnic minorities, and they want their children to have a better experience. TWI programs promote linguistic equity and balance through enrollment policies (balancing the number of native speakers of the program's two languages and including students with special needs), through the use of Spanish in school-wide activities and student assessment, and in the classroom through protection of Spanish instructional time. This also has the effect of meeting students' diverse needs, as program staff make choices about language allocation and about time and resources to be devoted to each language. Classroom teachers also find ways to make content comprehensible for language learners, while pushing native speakers to higher levels of proficiency. In so doing, they empower students to see their linguistic resources as an asset. Finally, TWI programs actively promote multicultural awareness and appreciation, both implicitly—by providing the opportunity for diverse students to learn from each other—and explicitly—by teaching about different countries and traditions. These phenomena are all infused throughout the program and the curriculum, and teachers and administrators understand that they are not optional even in this era of time-consuming state and federal mandates (Anberg-Espinosa, 2006). To promote a culture of equity to an even greater degree, teachers should explicitly discuss issues of diversity and power with students in developmentally appropriate ways (Brisk, 2006).

Leadership is about taking initiative based on perceived needs and problems, developing leadership in others, and valuing consensus building as a way to make decisions. Chapter 6 outlines several ways in which effective TWI programs manifest this type of leadership at the program and classroom levels. It begins with individual initiative and the presence of strong leaders who provide continuity for their program and who develop the talent of the rest of the staff through recruitment and professional development. Adults and students are encouraged to take ownership of their learning, while public presentation of work and ideas increases motivation, provides useful feedback, and improves confidence and self-esteem. Leaders also respond to the needs of others, such as when administrative staff take teachers' needs into consideration, or when they make peer support and consensus building a regular feature of their program and of classroom interaction.

The two extended examples in chapter 7 demonstrate not only how intellectualism, equity, and leadership play out in the context of classroom instruction, but also how activities at the classroom level can have program-level impact. They also demonstrate the need to incorporate many of the specific instructional strategies discussed in chapter 2 and elsewhere, such as thematic instruction, language and content integration, and cooperative learning. Working in cooperative groups to write sentences using new vocabulary words and engaging in higher order thinking about classification facilitate intellectualism; developing vocabulary, grammar, and writing skills in effective, contextualized ways that take students' backgrounds, interests, and learning styles into consideration promotes equity; and grouping students to facilitate peer mentoring and shared decision making encourages leadership. Likewise, at the program level, the teachers demonstrated intellectualism through their development of these approaches; they provided leadership by sharing their approaches with other teachers at their schools; and ultimately, as each approach gained popularity at the program level, they served to promote equity by improving Spanish Instruction and elevating the status of native Spanish speakers or by expanding multicultural instruction.

As practitioners reading this book work to promote bilingualism and biliteracy among the students in their own programs, they may find it useful to work through the study guide found in the appendix. This will help promote the reflective, process-oriented, and systemic approach suggested by the *Guiding Principles for Dual Language Education* (www.cal.org/twi/guidingprinciples.htm) and found in the four highly effective programs profiled in this book. Other useful tools for program-level and classroom-level reflection and improvement are the *Guiding Principles* themselves, as well as the *Two-Way Immersion Toolkit* and the many other books and resources listed on CAL's TWI Web site (www.cal.org/twi).

As we hope this book has made clear, the use of well-established strategies such as language and content integration, cooperative learning, and project-based instruction is crucial to the development of high levels of bilingualism and biliteracy among TWI students. The highly effective programs that we have worked with go a step further by using these strategies within the cultures of intellectualism, equity, and leadership at both the program and classroom levels. Teachers—as well as administrators and parents—are taken seriously as intellectuals; they work in environments that strive to promote equity with regard to the two languages of instruction and to the native speakers of those languages, and they capitalize on the diversity within their programs by fostering an appreciation for multiculturalism; and they are encouraged to take leadership roles in the school and in the larger TWI community. In addition, teachers are expected to develop the same cultures within their classrooms and to do so in ways that promote the development of high levels of bilingualism and biliteracy among both native Spanish speakers and native English speakers.

Moreover, effective programs develop and sustain these cultural norms systemically at both the program and classroom levels. Individuals engage in ongoing reflection, discussing student outcomes and ways that the program can work to improve itself. Taken together, these characteristics indicate a high level of respect for students, staff, and parents and encourage the collective empowerment of everyone involved. Fostering high levels of bilingualism and biliteracy among all students can be challenging, but as we have seen in this book, it is certainly possible when committed teachers, administrators, and parents come together to support student learning in an environment that empowers everyone through the cultures of intellectualism, equity, and leadership.

Postscript

A great deal has changed at the four focal programs in the years since our data collection. (The CREDE study collected longitudinal outcome data from 1997 to 2000 and qualitative data primarily from 2000 to 2002. The other two studies at Key, the teacher-researcher collaborative and the spelling study, were conducted from 1999 to 2001 and 2001 to 2005, respectively.)

These changes are both internally driven, such as Barbieri's reflection on its program model and Key's addition of a 30-minute Spanish language arts block, and externally driven, such as changes in staffing at the administrative level and in the demographics of the student population.

Of the four schools, only **Key** is still under the leadership of the principal (Marjorie Myers) and assistant principal (Evelyn Fernández) who were at the school during our periods of data collection, but the program has gone through some turnover in personnel at the school and district levels. First, the elementary TWI program in the district has expanded to a second whole-school site (in addition to the already-established secondary programs at a middle school and high school in the district), Claremont Immersion, and some teachers from Key are now teaching at Claremont in an effort to promote a strong, unified program across both schools. In addition, Marleny Perdomo, one of the veteran teachers interviewed for the study, has gone on to become the immersion coordinator for the district. However, the main change currently affecting Key is demographic. Because of rising housing costs in the area, which is located next to Washington, DC, many recent immigrants have moved to more distant suburbs, resulting in a reduced population of students who are dominant in Spanish. Although the ratio of Hispanic to non-Hispanic students at Key is still about 50/50, many of the Hispanic students are English dominant or balanced bilinguals. Unlike many communities in the United States, where the ELL population is growing, Arlington has seen the number of students qualifying for ESL-related services decrease over the past 4 years, as shown in Table 8.1.

Table 8.1: Percent of Students Qualifying for ESL Services at Key and in Arlington Public Schools (APS)

	2002	2003	2004	2005
Key Elementary School	41%	37%	35%	34%
APS – all elementary schools	33%	32%	30%	29%
APS – whole district	24%	23%	21%	20%

Source: Survey of Limited English Proficient Students, Arlington Public Schools Department of ESOL/HILT Instruction, September 2005

Because of these changes, Key and its sister elementary and secondary programs in the district are now looking at enrollment trends that move the model closer to foreign language immersion than TWI. Of course, both of these are types of dual language programs (Howard, Olague, et al., 2003), but Key staff now need to attend to issues that affect those "tweener" programs that straddle the line between foreign language immersion and TWI because of student population characteristics: for example, meeting the needs of native Spanish speakers in both English and Spanish when they make up a very small percentage of each classroom, avoiding native Spanish speaker burnout from overuse as translators, ensuring that linguistically and culturally diverse parents continue to have a strong voice in the school, and being sure that the philosophy and goals of the program, as well as teachers' instructional practices, are aligned with the realities of students' needs (Fortune & Tedick, 2006).

As discussed earlier, one additional change that Key has made is instituting a 30-minute daily language arts block in Spanish. This change was made in response to an increasing awareness that native speakers of both languages were struggling with some of the details of Spanish grammar and vocabulary, and in response to empirical evidence from the district's evaluation of the TWI program that showed a disparity between students' achievement in English and Spanish language arts (Forbes-Ullrich & Perdomo, 2005). Along the same lines, the program is working further in this area by developing and implementing a Spanish vocabulary intervention with assistance from the Center for Applied Linguistics.

The program at **Alicia Chacón** has remained the most consistent of the four focal programs since the time of data collection, in that it continues to employ a Spanish-dominant (80/10/10) model that includes initial literacy instruction in Spanish for all students and 10% of instruction through a third language at all grade levels. The school is divided into four families that correspond to the four different possible third languages (Mandarin Chinese, German, Japanese, or Russian), with each family having its own wing and its own administrator. The biggest change at Alicia Chacón over the past several years has been in its top administration. The founding principal, Bob Schulte, was reassigned to another school when the interim superintendent reassigned several principals in the district. This led to a period of unrest within the program, compounded by the untimely death of another founding administrator, Conchita Medina. The program now has its third principal and has stabilized from an administrative standpoint. Fortunately, there has been a great deal of staff continuity over the years—three of the four administrative heads of families have been at the school since the first or second year (the fourth original administrator is currently the coordinator of bilingual education for the district), and there has been relatively low teacher turnover. The other major change in the program is its expansion to a school-wide K–8 program, with a continuation program at several district high schools.

IAMS is currently feeling the effects of strong external forces that may incite permanent changes in this pioneering program. First, two key leaders are no longer with the program: Adela Greeley, a cofounder who taught at the school for many years and continued to provide guidance after her retirement, moved to Los Angeles, and longtime principal Eva Helwing retired. The Local School Council selected a new principal, but some teachers at the school felt left out of the process, creating some tension. Compounding this challenge is an even more pressing problem, the upcoming relocation of the school. Several years ago, IAMS was promised a new state-of-the-art school building, but before that promise could be fulfilled, the person at the district responsible for making it happen was replaced by someone with a different vision. The school will be moving to a refurbished, existing building as of the 2006–2007 school year, and the present building will be torn down. This is obviously an emotional experience for those who have been with the program for a long time, including many of the teachers and other staff.

Two factors throw the future of the program into question: (1) The school is moving to a neighborhood whose residents are primarily White, affluent, native English speakers; and (2) the court-ordered, district-wide policy providing busing to promote desegregation through the use of magnet schools may be abolished. While the district has agreed to provide transportation for all current students for the immediate future, it appears that, ultimately, the school will be serving a population that is primarily middle to upper class and Caucasian, causing it to face the foreign language immersion or tweener issues discussed for Key. Furthermore, a group of parents who are unhappy with the move are working to start a new program in a Hispanic neighborhood where the demographics are more similar to the school's current student profile, and some current IAMS teachers may seek to transfer to that program.

Barbieri and other TWI programs in Massachusetts have been able to continue implementing their programs despite passage of the November 2002 ballot initiative, Question 2, which prohibits most forms of bilingual education in the state except for TWI. As mentioned earlier, Barbieri is now under the leadership of one of its founding teachers, Minerva Gonzalez, after the retirement of its longtime principal, Peter Dittami, in 2001. Barbieri was one of the first programs to experiment with the TWI model, creating the differentiated program where students would first develop literacy and math skills in their native language, thus necessitating more separation of students into homogeneous language groups in the primary grades. After many years of reflection on this model, the program leadership has decided to move to an 80/20 model for fall 2007. They will be phasing in this change for the 2006–2007 school year by increasing the amount of Spanish instruction for native English speakers in kindergarten through Grade 2, so that all students will receive all instruction other than initial literacy instruction in Spanish in integrated groups. This change aims to increase the amount of Spanish instruction for the native English speakers and to improve the overall academic achievement of native Spanish speakers.

In summary, many of the changes that these four programs have experienced or are experiencing are indicative of the impact and unpredictability of external forces, such as demographic shifts, federal and district mandates, and political measures such as Question 2. These forces can make even well-established and strong programs, such as the four profiled here, vulnerable. It is the cultures of intellectualism, equity, and leadership in these schools that have enabled them to continue in turbulent times. As it is, some of the programs still have sizable challenges to face. It is to their credit that they continue to face these challenges; advocate for their programs at the school, district, and even national levels; and work for the good of the children they serve to realize the vision of two-way immersion.

References

Anberg-Espinosa, M. (2006, January). *Equity: The missing link in our two-way immersion programs.* Presentation at the National Association for Bilingual Education (NABE) Dual Language Immersion Pre-Conference Institute, Phoenix, AZ.

Bae, J., & Bachman, L. F. (1998). A latent variable approach to listening and reading: Testing factorial invariance across two groups of children in the Korean/English two-way immersion program. *Language Testing, 15*(3), 380–414.

Brisk, M. (2006). *Bilingual education: From compensatory to quality schooling* (2nd ed.). Mahwah, NJ: Erlbaum.

Brown, A. L., & Campione, J. C. (1994). Guided discovery in a community of learners. In K. McGilly (Ed.), *Classroom lessons: Integrating cognitive theory and classroom practice* (pp. 229–271). Cambridge, MA: MIT Press.

Calderón, M. E., & Minaya-Rowe, L. (2003). *Designing and implementing two-way bilingual programs: A step-by-step guide for administrators, teachers, and parents.* Thousand Oaks, CA: Corwin Press.

Carlo, M., August, D., McLaughlin, B., Snow, C., Dressler, D., Lippman, D., Lively, T., White, C. (2004). Closing the gap: Addressing the vocabulary needs of English language learners in bilingual and mainstream classrooms. *Reading Research Quarterly, 39,* 188–206.

Carrigo, D. L. (2000). *Just how much English are they using? Teacher and student language distribution patterns, between Spanish and English, in upper-grade, two-way immersion Spanish classes.* Unpublished doctoral dissertation, Harvard University, Cambridge, MA.

Carter, T., & Chatfield, M. (1986). Effective bilingual schools: Implications for policy and practice. *American Journal of Education, 95,* 200–232.

Caswell, L., & Howard, E. R. (2004, January). *Biliteracy development in two-way immersion and late-exit bilingual programs.* Featured presentation at the annual conference of the National Association for Bilingual Education, Albuquerque, NM.

Cazabon, M., Lambert, W. E., & Hall, G. (1993). *Two-way bilingual education: A progress report on the Amigos program* (Research Rep. No. 7). Santa Cruz, CA, and Washington, DC: National Center for Research on Cultural Diversity and Second Language Learning.

Center for Applied Linguistics. (2006). *Directory of two-way bilingual immersion programs in the U.S.* Retrieved February 6, 2006, from http://www.cal.org/twi/directory

Christian, D., Montone, C. L., Lindholm, K. J., & Carranza, I. (1997). *Profiles in two-way immersion education.* McHenry, IL, and Washington, DC: Delta Systems and Center for Applied Linguistics.

Cloud, N., Genesee, F., & Hamayan, E. (2000). *Dual language instruction: A handbook for enriched education.* Boston: Heinle & Heinle.

Cohen, E. G., & Lotan, R. A. (1995). Producing equal-status interaction in the heterogeneous classroom. *American Educational Research Journal, 32*(1), 99–120.

Cummins, J. (2006). *Rethinking monolingual instructional strategies in multilingual classrooms.* Paper presented at the annual conference of the American Association for Applied Linguistics, Montreal, Quebec, Canada.

Curtain, H., & Dahlberg, C. A. (2003). *Languages and children, making the match: New languages for young learners* (3rd ed.). Boston: Allyn & Bacon.

Dalton, S. S. (1998). *Pedagogy matters: Standards for effective teaching practice* (Research Rep. No. 4). Santa Cruz, CA, and Washington, DC: Center for Research on Education, Diversity & Excellence.

de Jong, E. J. (2002). Effective bilingual education: From theory to academic achievement in a two-way bilingual program. *Bilingual Research Journal, 26*(1), 65-84.

Delgado-Larocco, E. L. (1998). *Classroom processes in a two-way immersion kindergarten classroom.* Unpublished doctoral dissertation, University of California, Davis.

Echevarria, J., Vogt, M. E., & Short, D. (2004). *Making content comprehensible for English language learners: The SIOP Model* (2nd ed.). Boston: Allyn & Bacon.

Faltis, C. J., & Hudelson, S. J. (1998). *Bilingual education in elementary and secondary school communities: Toward understanding and caring.* Boston: Allyn & Bacon.

Forbes-Ullrich, M. A., & Perdomo, M. (2005). *Two-way immersion program evaluation report.* Arlington, VA: Arlington Public Schools.

Fortune, T. W., & Tedick, D. J. (2006, January). *"Tweeners": Issues and challenges in demographically-changing immersion programs.* Presentation at the NABE Dual Language Immersion Pre-Conference Institute, Phoenix, AZ.

Freeman, R. D. (1998). *Bilingual education and social change.* Clevedon, England: Multilingual Matters.

Freeman, Y. S., Freeman, D. E., & Mercuri, S. P. (2005). *Dual language essentials for teachers and administrators.* Portsmouth, NH: Heinemann.

García, E. (1993). Project THEME: Collaboration for school improvement at the middle school for language minority students. In National Clearinghouse for Bilingual Education (Ed.), *Proceedings of the Third National Research Symposium on Limited Proficiency Student Issues: Focus on middle and high school issues* (Vol. 1, pp. 323–350). Washington, DC: U.S. Department of Education, Office of Bilingual Education and Minority Languages Affairs.

Genesee, F. (1987). *Learning through two languages: Studies of immersion and bilingual education.* Cambridge, MA: Newbury.

Genesee, F. (1994). *Integrating language and content: Lessons from immersion* (Educational Practice Rep. No. 11). Santa Cruz, CA, and Washington, DC: National Center for Research on Cultural Diversity and Second Language Learning.

Genesee, F., Lindholm-Leary, K. J., Saunders, W., & Christian, D. (2006). *Educating English language learners: A synthesis of research evidence.* New York: Cambridge University Press.

Genesee, F., Paradis, J., & Crago, M. B. (2004). *Dual language development & disorders: A handbook on bilingualism and second language learning.* Baltimore: Brookes.

Glaser, B. G., & Strauss, A. L. (1967). *The discovery of grounded theory: Strategies for qualitative research.* Chicago: Aldine.

Glenn, C. (1990). How to integrate bilingual education without tracking: Best setting for linguistic minorities is school where two languages are used. *The School Administrator, 47*(5), 28–31.

Goldberg, M. (2001). *Lessons from exceptional school leaders.* Alexandria, VA: Association for Supervision and Curriculum Development.

Gort, M. (2001). *On the threshold of biliteracy: Bilingual writing processes of English-dominant and Spanish-dominant first graders in a two-way bilingual education program.* Unpublished doctoral dissertation, Boston University.

Griego-Jones, T. (1994). Assessing students' perceptions of biliteracy in two-way bilingual classrooms. *Journal of Educational Issues of Language Minority Students, 13,* 79–93.

Gumperz, J. J., Cook-Gumperz, J., & Szymanski, M. H. (1999). *Collaborative practices in bilingual cooperative learning classrooms* (Research Rep. No. 7). Santa Cruz, CA, and Washington, DC: Center for Research on Education, Diversity & Excellence.

Ha, J. H. (2001). *Elementary students' written language development in a Korean/English two-way immersion program.* Unpublished thesis, California State University, Long Beach.

Hadi-Tabassum, S. (2006). *Language, space, and power: A critical look at bilingual education.* Clevedon, England: Multilingual Matters.

Hancin-Bhatt, B., & Nagy, W. (1994). Lexical transfer and second language morphological development. *Applied Psycholinguistics, 15,* 289–310.

Howard, E. R. (2002). The Alicia Chacón International School: Portrait of an exemplary two-way immersion program. *NABE News, 25*(6), 19–22,42–43.

Howard, E. R. (2003). *Biliteracy development in two-way immersion education programs: A multilevel analysis of the effects of native language and home language use on the development of narrative writing ability in English and Spanish.* Unpublished doctoral dissertation, Harvard University, Cambridge, MA.

Howard, E. R., & Christian, D. (1997). *The development of bilingualism and biliteracy in two-way immersion students.* Paper presented at the annual meeting of the American Educational Research Association, Chicago.

Howard, E. R., & Christian, D. (2002). *Two-way immersion 101: Designing and implementing a two-way immersion education program at the elementary school level* (Educational Practice Rep. No. 9). Santa Cruz, CA, and Washington, DC: Center for Research on Education, Diversity & Excellence.

Howard, E. R., Christian, D., & Genesee, F. (2003). *The development of bilingualism and biliteracy from grade 3 to 5: A summary of findings from the CAL/CREDE study of two-way immersion education* (Research Rep. No. 13). Santa Cruz, CA, and Washington, DC: Center for Research on Education, Diversity & Excellence.

Howard, E. R., Lindholm-Leary, K., Sugarman, J., Christian, D., & Rogers, D. (2005). *Guiding principles for dual language education.* Washington, DC: Center for Applied Linguistics.

Howard, E. R., Olague, N., & Rogers, D. (2003). *The dual language program planner: A guide for designing and implementing dual language programs.* Santa Cruz, CA, and Washington, DC: Center for Research on Education, Diversity & Excellence.

Howard, E. R., Sugarman, J., & Christian, D. (2003). *Trends in two-way immersion education: A review of the research* (Report No. 63). Baltimore: Center for Research on the Education of Students Placed At Risk.

Howard, E. R., Sugarman, J., Perdomo, M., & Adger, C. T. (Eds.). (2005). The *two-way immersion toolkit.* Providence, RI: The Education Alliance at Brown University.

Howley, C. B., Howley, A., & Pendarvis, E. D. (1995). *Out of our minds: Anti-intellectualism and talent development in American schooling.* New York: Teachers College Press.

Jiménez, R. T., García, G. E., & Pearson, P. D. (1996). The reading strategies of bilingual Latino/a students who are successful English readers: Opportunities and obstacles. *Reading Research Quarterly, 31*(1), 283–301.

Kirk Senesac, B. V. (2002). Two-way bilingual immersion: A portrait of quality schooling. *Bilingual Research Journal, 26*(1), 85-101.

Kohn, A. (1999). *The schools our children deserve: Moving beyond traditional classrooms and "tougher standards."* Boston: Houghton Mifflin.

Levy, F., & Murnane, R. J. (2004). *The new division of labor: How computers are creating the next job market.* Princeton, NJ: Princeton University Press.

Lindholm, K. J. (1987). *Directory of bilingual immersion programs: Two-way bilingual education for language minority and majority students* (Educational Rep. No. 8). Los Angeles: Center for Language Education and Research.

Lindholm, K. J. (1990). Bilingual immersion education: Criteria for program development. In A. Padilla, H. Fairchild, & C. Valadez (Eds.), *Bilingual education: Issues and strategies* (pp. 91–105). Newbury Park, CA: Sage.

Lindholm-Leary, K. J. (2001). *Dual language education.* Clevedon, England: Multilingual Matters

Lindholm-Leary, K. J. (2005). *Review of research and best practices on effective features of dual language programs.* Retrieved February 6, 2006, from http://www.cal.org/twi/guidingprinciples.htm

Lindholm-Leary, K. J., & Howard, E. R. (in press). Language development and academic achievement in two-way immersion programs. In T. Fortune & D. Tedick (Eds.), *Pathways to multilingualism.* Clevedon, England: Multilingual Matters.

Lucas, T., Henze, R., & Donato, R. (1990). Promoting the success of Latino language minority students: An exploratory study of six high schools. *Harvard Educational Review, 60*(3), 315–340.

McCollum, P. (1999). Learning to value English: Cultural capital in a two-way bilingual program. *Bilingual Research Journal, 23*(2–3), 113–134

Nagy, W. E., García, G. E., Durgunoglu, A. Y., & Hancin-Bhatt, B. (1993). Spanish-English bilingual students' use of cognates in English reading. *Journal of Reading Behavior, 25,* 241–259.

National Center for Education Statistics. (2002). *Dropout rates in the United States: 2000.* Washington, DC: Author.

Olsen, L. (2005, July). *Making the third goal real: Building multicultural competency and relationships.* Presentation at the summer conference of 2-Way CABE, Monterey, CA.

Ortiz, A. A., & Yates, J. R. (2002). Considerations in the assessment of English language learners referred to special education. In A. J. Artiles & A. A. Ortiz (Eds.), *English language learners with special education needs: Identification, assessment, and instruction* (pp. 65–86). Washington, DC, and McHenry, IL: Center for Applied Linguistics and Delta Systems.

Pérez, B. (2004). *Becoming biliterate: A study of two-way bilingual immersion education.* Mahwah, NJ: Erlbaum.

Potowski, K. (2002). *Language use in a dual immersion classroom: A sociolinguistic perspective.* Unpublished doctoral dissertation, University of Illinois, Urbana-Champaign.

Pressley, M. (2002). *Reading instruction that works: The case for balanced teaching* (2nd ed.). New York: Guilford Press.

Resnick, L. B., & Hall, M. W. (2005). *Principles of learning for effort-based education.* Pittsburgh, PA: Institute for Learning, Learning Research and Development Center.

Rhodes, N. C., Christian, D., & Barfield, S. (1997). Innovations in immersion: The Key School two-way model. In R. K. Johnson & M. Swain (Eds.), *Immersion education: International perspectives* (pp. 265–283). New York: Cambridge University Press.

Rogoff, B., Matusov, E., & White, C. (1996). Models of teaching and learning: Participation in a community of learners. In D. Olson & N. Torrance (Eds.), *The handbook of education and human development: New models of learning, teaching, and schooling* (pp. 388–414). Cambridge, MA: Blackwell.

Saunders, W., & O'Brien, G. (2006). Oral language. In F. Genesee, K. J. Lindholm-Leary, W. Saunders, & D. Christian (Eds.), *Educating English language learners: A synthesis of research evidence* (pp. 14–63). New York: Cambridge University Press.

Slavin, R. (1995). *Cooperative learning: Theory, research, and practice* (2nd ed.). Boston: Allyn & Bacon.

Soltero, S. W. (2004). *Dual language: Teaching and learning in two languages.* Boston: Allyn & Bacon.

Stringfield, S., Datnow, A., & Ross, S. M. (1998). *Scaling up school restructuring in multicultural, multilingual contexts: Early observations from Sunland County* (Research Rep. No. 2). Santa Cruz, CA, and Washington, DC: Center for Research on Education, Diversity & Excellence.

Sugarman, J., & Howard, E. R. (2001). *Development and maintenance of two-way immersion programs: Advice from practitioners* (Practitioner Brief No. 2). Santa Cruz, CA, and Washington, DC: Center for Research on Education, Diversity & Excellence.

Swain, M. (1996). Integrating language and content in immersion classrooms: Research perspectives. *Canadian Modern Language Review, 52*(4), 529–548.

Tharp, R., & Gallimore, R. (1988). *Rousing minds to life: Teaching, learning, and schooling in social context.* New York: Cambridge University Press.

Thomas, W. P., & Collier, V. (1997). *School effectiveness for language minority students.* Washington, DC: National Clearinghouse for Bilingual Education.

Thomas, W. P., & Collier, V. (2002). *A national study of school effectiveness for language minority students' long-term academic achievement: Final report.* Santa Cruz, CA, and Washington, DC: Center for Research on Education, Diversity & Excellence.

Thompson, L., Boyson, B., & Rhodes, N. (2001). *Student Oral Proficiency Assessment (SOPA) administrator's manual.* Washington, DC, and Ames, IA: Center for Applied Linguistics and Iowa State University National K–12 Foreign Language Resource Center.

Urow, C., & Sontag, J. (2001). Creating community—Un mundo entero: The Inter-American experience. In D. Christian & F. Genesee (Eds.), *Bilingual education* (pp. 11–26). Alexandria, VA: Teachers of English to Speakers of Other Languages.

Vygotsky, L. S. (1978). *Mind in society.* Cambridge, MA: Harvard University Press.

Woodcock, R. W. (1991). *Woodcock language proficiency battery-revised (WLPB-R).* Itasca, IL: Riverside.

Woodcock, R. W., & Muñoz-Sandoval, A. F. (1991). *Woodcock language proficiency battery-revised, Spanish form.* Itasca, IL: Riverside.

Zucker, C. (1995). The role of ESL in a dual language program. *Bilingual Research Journal, 19*(3&4), 513–523.

Appendix: Study Guide

One way to put the ideas in this book into practice is to form teacher study groups to discuss both the theoretical ideas and practical implications of the cultures of intellectualism, leadership, and equity for TWI programs The questions in this study guide are intended to stimulate discussion about each chapter and to form a basis for reflection about present practices and plans for future growth.

Study groups are generally school-based and focus discussion on the local context. They typically have 6–12 participants and meet fairly regularly, for example, once or twice a month. Groups should be run democratically, with all members defining expectations, participating actively, and promoting sustained learning by making connections and proposing follow-up with other professional development activities. Study group sessions can be led by a group member who is a skilled facilitator or by each participant taking a turn. (For more guidelines on starting a study group and discussing professional literature, see Howard, Sugarman, et al., 2005.)

In addition to addressing the questions proposed here for each chapter, participants might want to compare views by listing issues from the chapter that pertain to their own experiences and posing open-ended questions about them, such as these:

- What does the reading have to say on the topic?
- Do you agree with the reading? What evidence supports your opinion?
- How have you dealt with this issue?

Before closing the discussion, facilitators may want to ask the group to share any new questions they have as a result of talking about the reading, or to identify additional work that may need to be done in the school to address the issues that were raised.

Chapter 1: Setting the Context

Prereading Discussion

1. What are the features and demographics of your program? How do you think they might impact other aspects of the program, such as curriculum, instruction, and family and community involvement?
2. What do you know about research on TWI programs in terms of the different models used throughout the country and the outcomes that have been found in existing programs?

Postreading Discussion

1. The authors provide a summary of TWI research on academic achievement, literacy, and integration of language minority and language majority students. To what degree does your program mirror those findings?
2. In this chapter, the authors identify three important qualities that distinguish highly effective programs: reflection, a process orientation, and a system-wide approach. To what extent does your program have these three characteristics? Why do you think this is the case?
3. The chapter concludes by stating that cultures of intellectualism, equity, and leadership are the larger contextual pieces essential for effective programs and the promotion of high levels of bilingualism and biliteracy. What predictions do you have about the features of each one of these cultures and why they may be important for promoting bilingualism and biliteracy development?

Chapter 2: Approaches to Instruction for Bilingualism and Biliteracy

Prereading Discussion

1. What does your program model look like? What approach does your program use for initial literacy instruction?
2. What are the most important issues in language and literacy development in your program?
3. What strategies do you use to promote bilingualism and biliteracy in your program?

Postreading Discussion

1. Do teachers in your program use all of the instructional strategies identified in the chapter? Which strategies do you find most useful? Which are most challenging?
2. What does a balanced approach to literacy instruction mean to you? Does your program use a balanced approach? If so, what does it look like? If not, why not?
3. One of the central issues in TWI instruction is the need to respond to both first and second language learners in two languages. The four focal programs deal with this through the combined use of homogenous and heterogeneous groupings, but each program uses these groupings differently. How does your program respond to this issue? What are the benefits of separating students by language dominance versus working with heterogeneous groups?
4. Having high expectations for students is another hallmark of TWI education. Consider this statement made by an upper elementary teacher at IAMS: "We shoot higher than the kids' ability and then we support the kids to reach that level." Do you agree with this philosophy? If so, what do you do to support the students to perform above their ability levels? If not, why not?

Chapter 3: Bilingualism and Biliteracy Attainment in Two-Way Immersion Programs

Prereading Discussion

1. What types of student outcome data does your program collect? How often do you collect it?
2. What are the areas of greatest concern in your program regarding students' bilingualism and biliteracy development?

Postreading Discussion

1. What benefit is there to looking at longitudinal data? At comparative data across schools or districts?
2. How do your student outcomes in oral language, reading, and writing compare to those of the four focal programs? What do you find to be your students' greatest strengths and biggest challenges?
3. How do your native English speakers and native Spanish speakers compare on measures in English and Spanish? If this is different from the trends reported in our research and in the literature, why do you think that is?

Chapter 4: Promoting Bilingualism and Biliteracy Through a Culture of Intellectualism

Prereading Discussion

1. What do you think are the features of a culture of intellectualism? Do you consider your program to have a culture of intellectualism? Why or why not?
2. How could a culture of intellectualism promote bilingualism and biliteracy attainment?

Postreading Discussion

1. Is your program characterized by an atmosphere of ongoing learning? Is there reflection and change, an attitude that it's OK to make mistakes, and high expectations for everyone? Is this true at the program and classroom levels? If so, why? If not, why not?
2. Is there collaboration and an exchange of ideas in your program, and does this happen at the program and classroom levels? If so, why? If not, why not?
3. Is independence fostered in your program, and does this happen at the program and classroom levels? If so, why? If not, why not?
4. Is higher order thinking promoted in your program, and does this happen at the program and classroom levels? If so, why? If not, why not?
5. Do you agree that the previous four components are indicators of a culture of intellectualism? Why or why not? What other indicators might there be?
6. Do you agree that a culture of intellectualism can help promote bilingualism and biliteracy? Why or why not?

Chapter 5: Promoting Bilingualism and Biliteracy Through a Culture of Equity

Prereading Discussion

1. What do you think are the features of a culture of equity? Do you consider your program to have a culture of equity? Why or why not?
2. How could a culture of equity promote bilingualism and biliteracy attainment?

Postreading Discussion

1. Does your program value and protect time for the partner language and culture? Is this true at the program and classroom levels? If so, why? If not, why not?
2. Does your program promote bilingualism for students with special needs? Is this true at the program and classroom levels? If so, why? If not, why not?
3. Does your program balance the needs of native English speakers and native Spanish speakers? Is this true at the program and classroom levels? If so, why? If not, why not?
4. Does your program foster an appreciation for multiculturalism through diversity in the school and culture in the curriculum? Is this true at the program and classroom levels? If so, why? If not, why not?
5. Do you agree that the previous four components are indicators of a culture of equity? Why or why not? What other indicators might there be?
6. Do you agree that a culture of equity can help promote bilingualism and biliteracy? Why or why not?

Chapter 6: Promoting Bilingualism and Biliteracy Through a Culture of Leadership

Prereading Discussion

1. What do you think are the features of a culture of leadership? Do you consider your program to have a culture of leadership? Why or why not?

2. How could a culture of leadership promote bilingualism and biliteracy attainment?

Postreading Discussion

1. Do individuals take initiative in your program, and does this happen at the program and classroom levels? If so, why? If not, why not?

2. Is public presentation a common occurrence in your program, and does this happen at the program and classroom levels? If so, why? If not, why not?

3. Do individuals in your program respond to the needs of others, and does this happen at the program and classroom levels? If so, why? If not, why not?

4. Is there consensus building and shared leadership in your program, and does this happen at the program and classroom levels? If so, why? If not, why not?

5. Do you agree that the previous four components are indicators of a culture of leadership? Why or why not? What other indicators might there be?

6. Do you agree that a culture of leadership can help promote bilingualism and biliteracy? Why or why not?

Chapter 7: What Does It Look Like? Intellectualism, Equity, and Leadership in Practice

Prereading Discussion

1. What do you consider to be the essential elements in any approach that aims to foster bilingualism and biliteracy?
2. How effective do you consider the approaches that are currently in use in your program?

Postreading Discussion

1. How does Ivonne Govea's approach help foster the Spanish writing development of her students? How could this approach be modified for instruction in English or in the upper grades?
2. How does Cheryl and Jill's approach help promote bilingualism and biliteracy attainment? Do you agree with the way that they integrate instruction across both languages within a given content theme? Why or why not?
3. Could you envision using either or both of these approaches in your classroom? What modifications might you need to make and why?
4. What are some other possible approaches for promoting bilingualism and biliteracy development?

Chapter 8: Putting It All Together

Prereading Discussion

1. What have you taken away from reading this book? How would you summarize the cultures of intellectualism, equity, and leadership at the four focal schools?

Postreading Discussion

1. What are some of the internally driven changes that have been made in your program? How do you think they affect the program as a whole? What additional issues within your program do you need to reflect on and review as a result?

2. What are some of the external forces that have affected your program? How do you think they affect the program as a whole? What additional issues within your program do you need to reflect on and review as a result? How can you advocate at the local, state, or national level for the needs of your program and your students?

About the Authors

Elizabeth Howard

Elizabeth Howard is an assistant professor of bilingual education in the Neag School of Education at the University of Connecticut. Previously, she was a senior research associate with the Center for Applied Linguistics (CAL), where she directed a number of projects related to biliteracy development and dual language education. She has authored several publications on dual language education and is the co-creator of a variety of resources for dual language programs, including *Guiding Principles for Dual Language Education,* The *Dual Language Program Planner,* and The *Two-Way Immersion Toolkit.* She also worked as a bilingual elementary school teacher in California and taught adult ESL and literacy courses as a Peace Corps Volunteer in Costa Rica.

Julie Sugarman

Julie Sugarman is a research associate at the Center for Applied Linguistics. She has been involved in research on the biliteracy development of students in two-way immersion (TWI) programs and has helped to create and disseminate a variety of online resources for TWI educators, including the *Directory of Two-Way Bilingual Immersion Programs in the U.S.* and the *Two-Way Immersion Toolkit.* Her current focus is on dual language program development and evaluation, which includes helping schools use the *Guiding Principles for Dual Language Education* as a tool for program improvement. She has presented at numerous national conferences and is working toward a Ph.D. in second language education and culture.